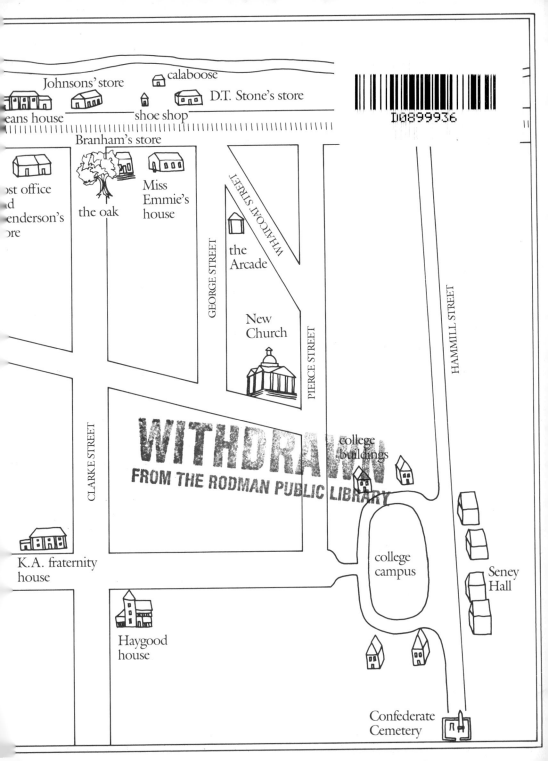

Johnsons' store

calaboose

D.T. Stone's store

eans house

shoe shop

Branham's store

st office
d
enderson's
re

the oak

Miss
Emmie's
house

GEORGE STREET

WHATCOAT STREET

the
Arcade

New
Church

PIERCE STREET

HAMMILL STREET

CLARKE STREET

college
buildings

college
campus

Seney
Hall

K.A. fraternity
house

Haygood
house

Confederate
Cemetery

The Blessed
Town

American Places of the Heart

Sea Island Yankee, by Clyde Bresee
The Blessed Town: Oxford, Georgia, at the Turn of the Century, by Polly Stone Buck

The Blessed Town

Oxford, Georgia, at the Turn of the Century

Polly Stone Buck

Algonquin Books of Chapel Hill
1986

published by
Algonquin Books of Chapel Hill
Post Office Box 2225
Chapel Hill, North Carolina 27515-2225

in association with

Taylor Publishing Company
1550 West Mockingbird Lane
Dallas, Texas 75235

Illustrations by Anna E. Birkner

LIBRARY OF CONGRESS CATALOGING-IN-PUBLICATION DATA
Buck, Polly Stone.
The blessed town.

(American places of the heart)
1. Buck, Polly Stone. 2. Oxford (Ga.)—Biography.
3. Oxford (Ga.)—Social life and customs.
I. Title. II. Series.
F294.O93B83   1986   975.8'593   86-3482
ISBN 0−912697−38−5

Dedicated to my gallant mother and
to my two brothers,
who both turned out all right.
One became an attorney and
the other a vice-president for Ma Bell.

No spot on earth has so helped to form and make what I am as this town of Oxford.

—JUSTICE L. Q. C. LAMAR 1870
Emory Class of 1845

Contents

Illustrations

Preface

This is a tale of people and events in the village of Oxford, Georgia, when Emory College, then only a small school of a few hundred male students, was located there. Most of it happened at the beginning of the twentieth century in what might be called the B.C. years—*Before Coca-Cola* millions moved the little country college to Atlanta and made it into the present great university.

The narrator, an Emory faculty daughter, was unaware of the precarious financial situation in which her father's sudden death from pneumonia had left her family, and from that long-ago perspective rattles on happily about what seems to her the idyllic life that everyone in the town led.

There must have been other homes besides hers (especially among the Negroes, who made up almost half of the population) where "idyllic" was not the appropriate word—but little Florrie Stone, blissfully ignorant of this, skipped along the dirt sidewalks to grammar school and to Sunday school, and in the afternoons to other little girls' homes to play paper dolls or Flinch. On rainy days, curled up with a book, she watched the drops splash against the window panes and dreamed of the possibility that she was really a princess and might any day be summoned out of Oxford to fill her rightful role.

During those first ten years of the twentieth century, Oxford seemed indeed a peaceable kingdom. Wars were "old, forgotten far-off things" in history books, and everyone was convinced that there would never be another; why, there was not even "unrest" anywhere! God was definitely on the job in His heaven, not too far away from Oxford, and all was right with the world.

P. S. B.

The Blessed
Town

I

A Place Set Apart

My young widowed mother and I were both slender and could sit together in one big porch rocking chair. The little village lay quiet around us in the moonlight.

We had been singing, as we frequently did on summer nights on the porch, songs Mother had known as a girl, and some of my favorites from Sunday school—"A hieland laddie there lived o'er the way," "Oh, that beautiful city with its mansions of light!" My two brothers were about their own affairs—fifteen-year-old Lowrey at the dining room table decoding spy messages under the big kerosene student lamp; Harry, thirteen, in the porch swing at some girl's house, to ramble home, whistling, about nine o'clock.

This was a typical summer evening for us, and all over Oxford other families were spending it in the same way—grown people and children sitting together on the cool porch, rocking and talking, a gentleman caller perhaps dropping by if there was a pretty girl in the family, to share the gently moving swing with her.

I was about seven or eight, knowing no troubles of my own, and having no idea that there were any such. But indeed there were; my own mother had plenty of them, although I never knew, for we were extremely poor, since there was no longer a father's faculty salary. The only money coming in was from a few college boarders ("between five and six boys," as Mother once expressed it)—and not even this during the long summer vacations—and from the small, unpredictable sums Mother might make by "sewing for people." There were no paying jobs for women outside the home except for the four teachers at Palmer Institute, our school. Oxford women were occupied in the non-remunerative business of being faculty wives, for practically every head of a family taught or worked at the college; nobody ever forgot for a minute that education was the "glorious business" for which the town had been founded.

Towns usually grow gradually, their winding streets originally determined by the paths along which the first settlers' cows had chosen to walk between barn and creek, but not ours! Oxford was not laid out by strolling cows; it was an early example of city planning, our straight streets marked on a drawing-board by a skilled engineer before the first shovelful of dirt was lifted.

This is how it all happened.

As a younger, less lettered part of the country, Georgia had looked to its older sister, Virginia, for its culture, contributing every year to Virginia's colleges, both financially and by sending its sons there to be educated. But in or about 1838, a few well-heeled Georgia Methodists had the idea of keeping both money and sons at home by building their own college.

They found a desirable site forty miles south of Atlanta, with invigorating air, pure water, and magnificent stands of pines and hardwoods. The original Indian owners had recently been moved west, so 1,452 acres of the empty land were purchased for $14,950, and here the town of Oxford and Emory College had a twin birth, springing into the world like Minerva, full-grown, for homes for its teachers must also be built; on the newly bought wilderness location there was at that time only one log cabin. A well-known architect and engineer, Edward Lloyd Thomas, who had recently gained notice by solving the boundary problems of the little city of Columbus, Georgia, was hired to plan both the new college and a town of faculty residences.

Oxford's founders were high-minded men, and their idea for the new college and town was to be "a place set apart, pervaded by an atmosphere of culture and science, devoted solely to the glorious business of education and religion." It was also to be a little modern Eden, where no evil thing would ever enter. The town's charter stipulated that alcohol or gambling of any sort was never to be allowed to cross the town line. Although the world, the flesh, and the devil might pace the boundaries, and lash forked tails in thwarted despair of such tender prey as Methodist college students would afford, they did not dare step over the town limits. Doubtless some of the students, bending over books, or sweating at wholesome sports, or even some of the younger faculty might cast a wishful eye over a shoulder occasionally, but it was never common knowledge, and whole generations of faculty children were to grow up without even knowing that such things existed.

Not only were there to be no worldly pleasures to distract the young men's minds, but there was to be in the town no money-getting of any sort, no commercial enterprise, no industry, no "stigma of trade."

The master of ceremonies at Bath once told Mr. Pickwick that "the reason the ball nights there were snatched from paradise, was chiefly because of the absence of trade people, who are quite inconsistent with paradise." If that be true, then Oxford was certainly planned as an earthly paradise. Thoughts were to be focused on things of the mind and soul, not on buying and selling and worldly profit. Was there ever, anywhere in the world, such a piece of perfection as this village? Oxonians proudly thought not.

They were certainly a pious and erudite group. Few of them knew the price of a bushel of anything, or even how many beans make five, but most could take up a book in Greek or Latin and read it as easily as if it were in English. They were contented inmates of their little ivory tower, and zealously endeavored to impart a Christian, classical education to their young charges, keeping them in the process unspotted from the world.

Almost everybody in town had a title; "everybody" meant only the men, of course. Since the women were all just wives, their title was "Mrs.," although the children and the black folks would use their given names when addressing them, preceded by "Mis'"— Mis' Mary, Mis' Addie, etc. Several of the older and more devout church members still called each other "Sister" and "Brother." My grandmother Lowrey always spoke of church members in this way, and she in turn was usually called "Sister Lowrey," but to do so was considered very "old-timey," and was not done by the younger, more up-and-coming generation. There were a number of Ph.D.'s and doctors of divinity among the men, and when we addressed them, we always prefixed "Doctor." If a man had ever studied law—my father, for instance—he was ever afterward called "Colonel." If there were no other title to use, we prefixed "Professor" ('Fessa). There were very few plain Misters in Oxford. "Aunt" and "Uncle" were used by both white and black when addressing the older black people.

My mother, my two older brothers, and I lived in Oxford for several reasons. First, because that was where we were living when my father died, and we simply stayed on. Second, because as the center of the universe, it was naturally the place to live—probably everyone who could live here did so. And third, because we had nowhere else to go. In the beginning, we had stayed in the old home where my father was raised, one of the earliest and loveliest houses in Oxford, built for his own use by the man who laid out the town and college. But when my aged grandmother, who had been staying with her daughter in Atlanta largely because of her

The Stone House

furnace-heated house, wanted to come back, we had to leave. My grandmother couldn't have stood the noise that my brothers made (Mother sometimes thought *she* couldn't); and Grandmother had been displeased with Mother for renting the extra bedrooms to college boys. The *family* was always welcome there, but to have men who were no kin in the house, and *paying for it* too, Grandmother thought was not desirable. For money to change hands Grandmother thought smacked too much of *trade* (their room rent was the only cash my mother had).

So Mother borrowed enough for a down payment, and bought the old Griffin place, nearer to the college, so that students would be easier to get, especially if she fed them, too.

2

The Griffin Place

There is now a state historical marker in front of this house, not because *we* lived in it, but because it had been in 1864 the hiding place of a Confederate girl spy. When we lived there, the town was not so historically minded as it became later, though of course everyone knew the story.

It was one of the earliest houses built in the town; I liked that. "In the beginning" is a magical phrase not only in the first verse of Genesis. Even as a girl of six I was proud of the fact that this house and the Thomas-Stone house where we had previously lived were two of the first to be built. When most of Oxford had been only staked-off lots and piles of lumber, there was already smoke curling from our chimneys, and families established inside—my grandfather's family in the Thomas-Stone house. It was a harmless sort of small-town snobbery—something like being proud that an ancestor had come over on the *Mayflower*, even though the one who made the trip might have been a leather-aproned cooper or a wheelwright.

The Griffin place had been a substantial home for many years, although never as elegant as the Thomas-Stone house, but owners toward the end of the century had neglected it, and it was only because of its rundown condition that my mother was able to afford to buy it. Its valuation on the town property list was $1,370, and her tax for 1907 was $6.17.

Originally the clapboards had been white, but so many summer Georgia suns had blistered the paint since the last coat was put on, and so many winter rains had lashed it, that it was now a rather indeterminate gray, almost at the state called "weathered," a term applied when there had never been any paint at all.

Its grounds and plan were more or less typical of the not-too-well-to-do Oxford homes. Downstairs were three halls and six rooms, with two more small bedrooms up a steep flight of stairs beneath the slanting roof. We had four college boys living in the two biggest downstairs bedrooms, and one each in the upstairs rooms.

There was about an acre of land altogether, with quite a large yard on one side, and behind it Mother set out several peach trees. How lovely her little orchard was when it bloomed in the spring! "The peach trees washed their branches in pink suds." Back yards were purely for use, not for show. There was a whitewashed chicken-house and a little wire-enclosed fowl-yard, a lackadaisical pyramidal pile of wood cut for the kitchen range, a potato patch, and a good-sized garden. The word "garden" always meant vegetables; flowers were planted out in front in "beds." Mother had a rose bed of about a dozen bushes; a crepe myrtle bush stood near the porch; and the walk from the porch to the street was bordered with violets and white clove pinks.

A high wooden paling fence encircled the garden, and the little boy who lived next door and I walked miles on its top rail, arms outstretched for balance, placing one foot carefully before the other. Anyone who toppled off, which happened often, for the rail was narrow, had to start all over again from the gate. "Uncle" Frank Brown, a black man, came to take care of the garden. He was very old, and had done hard outdoor labor all of his life, with the result that his big hands looked as if he were wearing a pair of leather gloves. I once saw him lift a live coal with his bare fingers to light his corncob pipe.

A very old cedar tree stood on each side of the house out in front. Harry immediately staked out a claim for the larger, and he and his two pals built a tree house. It was just a platform of old boards, with croker sack curtains rigged around it for privacy and a knotted rope hanging down for climbing. This insured against any intrusion by a sister, for girls did not shinny up ropes—our skirts would fly up. I often settled myself underneath while the boys huddled over my head, occasionally parting the curtain and looking over the edge to make hideous faces at me by pulling their eyes down and their mouths up, sticking out their tongues, and telling me crossly, "Twenty-three, skidoo, kid!"

In the large side yard the boys made a tennis court; it was not up to Wimbledon standards, for although it had the correct proportions, taken meticulously from a Spalding guide, the surface was only hard bare dirt with the grass scraped off with a hoe, and the boundary lines had to be re-marked with a stick before each game. Occasionally a thread of lime, extracted from the bucket in the privy, was dribbled along them. A net was a necessity, and Sears Roebuck sold them for from 65 cents to $2.15, but backstops were frills, so there were none, and players spent about as much time retrieving balls as swinging at them. After each ball was knocked out there was a pause in the playing while every eye followed to see where it wound up. For once, my brothers considered me an asset, for I was ball-chaser-in-chief. I was just young enough, and silly enough, to think it a privilege to be allowed to run myself breathless all afternoon chasing the balls they had swatted off the court. Any little girls who came over to play with me were allowed to chase them, too.

At the very extreme back of our lot was the well. (Two other wells, nearer the house and therefore more convenient, had in past

The Griffin House

years gone dry and had to be filled in.) It had a waist-high wooden frame with a roof, since a great round hole fifteen feet deep with water at the bottom couldn't be left unwalled and unroofed to look up at the stars and have people and animals, not to mention trash and leaves, constantly falling in to foul it. When you leaned over the frame and looked into it, far, far away at the bottom you could see daylight, and your own head outlined against it. When the empty bucket went down, if you stood well out of the way of the flying iron handle, you could let the windlass go, and watch it spin madly around until a great plop far below told you the bucket had hit. Then came the slow and heavy job of winding it back up on a windlass polished smooth and shining with much use.

On opposite sides of the back yard were two privies, a good long way from the house, and on a rainy or cold night the way seemed even longer. The men's was screened appropriately by a large fig tree, with branches to the ground; the women's starkly unhidden by any greenery, or even a lattice screen, which most privies usually had. The path to it led nowhere else, so on my way there, there was no question where I was bound, and when I was ready to come out, if anybody should be engaged in any occupation in the back yard, such as splitting kindling or carrying in coal scuttles, I was a prisoner inside until they went away, for it took more brass than a timid little girl possessed to come out of that door in the face of spectators.

These "necessary houses" all over the town were just alike, in that they had no windows and were close, dark little places where you had to leave the door half open for light. They were of the most primitive construction with no foundation, and could easily be pushed over, which the rough older boys delighted to do on Halloween night raids.

In ours, besides a bucket of fireplace ashes, we also kept a bucket of unslaked lime, from which to deposit a shovelful through the hole when you left. I was always in terror that some of it would spill on the side of the seat and eat into my flesh the next time I came. Another hazard to my vivid imagination was a bite from one of the spiders that built their webs underneath the seats. Clay nests of dirt daubers were plastered against the rafters overhead, but although they looked like wasps, they were harmless and never came down to bother you. Always visible through the seats' holes were hideous iridescent bronze-green flies, which you prayed would leave you alone and light somewhere else than on your tender little bottom.

There was no toilet paper, but we carried down the old Sears Roebuck catalogue, tissue paper patterns discarded after Mother's sewing, and the Atlanta newspapers. Children took a fiendish delight in "wiping off" with the pictures of ladies in the Sunday society pages. Even the best-kept of these little houses smelled horrid; as little time as possible was spent inside; there was no settling down to read the newspaper.

Trips after dark to the privies were made with a kerosene lantern always kept filled on the back porch shelf, to light the path and the interior, since nobody wanted to walk in on a raccoon or a polecat that had taken sanctuary for the night.

Inside our house ran three separate halls in a row, into which the four downstairs bedrooms, the sitting room, and the dining room opened. The hall ceilings were too low for throwing balls, alas, but grounders often rumbled all the way down their bare floors on a rainy day. (And playing catch outside *over* the house was a great sport for the boys. I couldn't begin to throw that high, but I was a delighted spectator; seeing the ball suddenly appear in the sky over the ridgepole was exciting; then the catcher had to figure out just where to move so that the ball would land in his glove.)

The first hall was a little one, with the stairs going up from it, and the door opening into the sitting room, which was not grand enough to be called a parlor. In here, the mantelpiece was draped with a length of printed voile, looped up in three or four places, and right in the center sat a long, shining black clock—a wedding present. It had lions' paw feet, and on each end the head of a lion holding a brass ring in its mouth.

There was very little furniture: only a small center table for the lamp, some chairs—one that was known as "Father's chair," and rockers that went out on the porch in the summer—and our library, such as it was, in a couple of bookcases with glass doors. We had eight volumes of the *Encyclopedia Brittanica* (for whose later edition one of my Oxford cousins, then a little girl in a pinafore at Palmer Institute, would one day write the definitive article on meningitis), and a set of the *Book of Knowledge* that my mother, terrified at raising boys without a father, had bought on the installment plan from a persuasive college boy book agent, who assured her it would "answer all the questions her children would ask."

There was one really beautiful book, to be looked at only with freshly washed hands. It was a large two-volume edition of Shakespeare that my father had been given by his great-aunt Tadie of Charleston on his graduation from Emory. The print was blinding small, but the illustrations were by Phiz, hand-colored and piercingly lovely. There were several other shelves of books of poetry or one thing and another, and a complete set of Dickens, on very poor paper with no illustrations, which my parents had bought to read aloud in the evenings the first year they were married.

There were few children's books in print then, and we owned only a few of the few—gifts from aunts and uncles at Christmas. The boys had *Swiss Family Robinson, Black Beauty, Beautiful Joe, Little Lord Fauntleroy*, the *Deerslayer* books, and one about wild animals, with pictures that were both interesting and terrifying. A lion was holding down a "native" in his paws; a great wildcat of some sort, with little bunches of hair growing on the tips of his pointed ears, was crouched on a tree limb about to jump on a little boy walking all unaware underneath. (As a result, I often would look up apprehensively into trees, especially if I were alone.) Wringing children's withers was perfectly good sport for book publishers.

I had a few girl-books: *Diddie, Dumps, and Tot, Little Lucy's Wonderful Globe, Little Susie's Six Birthdays*, and three of Andrew Lang's fairy books.

In the big square center hall, Mother kept the trunks and blanket chests. It was floored with wide boards, and through the cracks between them you could see the ground underneath. We dropped any broken machine needles through as interment in a place where they could do no harm. You can imagine how the cold air came up those cracks in the winter.

The back hall, off which the dining room opened, was long and narrow. The dining table, elongated with several leaves, just about filled the room. After supper every night the white tablecloth was taken off and a dark-green heavy one with a fringe put on, and here my brothers and I did our lessons by the light of the lamp set in the middle of the table, while Mother darned stockings within supervising and helping distance. (Children wore heavy black ribbed cotton stockings, and the darning basket was always piled high.) Matching the table was a golden oak sideboard with wooden curlicues, a beveled mirror across the top, and cupboards underneath, bought by my parents in the first exuberant flush of being married and setting up housekeeping. The pictures on the walls were two oil paintings, one of a luscious cut watermelon sitting on a fringed napkin, and one of a basket of purple grapes, both considered extremely appropriate for a dining room, and both from the decidedly amateur brush of my aunt Judith, who would try anything.

This back hall lay directly under the place where the two side gables of the roof came down into a sort of gully, roofed with tin. We had been in the house only a few weeks when there came a stormy night, and all the rain that came down both of the gable sides collected here, and then streamed through the hall ceiling. One receptacle after another was hurriedly brought, as the water dripped through in new places, until we had at least eight pans and buckets standing around, and in each one a resounding plunk, plunk, ker-plunk keeping up an antiphonal chorus. Listening to the rain in the night on a tin roof when you are in a snug house is a pleasant thing, but the sound was not so poetic when eight buckets were rapidly filling from leaks, and there was no idea where the money for a new roof could be found.

And it had to be found, for the back hall was not the only place where the rain seeped through. The shingles on the whole house, which had been put on evidently in some ancient year, were spongy rotten, and before college boys could be lured into coming to board, the roof *had* to be made tight. Somehow, Mother managed it, although of course it sank her deeper in debt. A scrap of paper in her handwriting gave the figures:

Shingles, nails, etc.	104.62
Work	22.69
total	$127.31

This was a horrendous sum for her.

It was great fun to have scaffolding circling the house, and after the workmen went home in the afternoons the boy from next door and I had a good time climbing around on it. Mother came home from a missionary meeting late one day to be joyfully hailed by the two of us, sitting on the ridgepole. I was seven, he five.

As the men ripped off the rotten old shingles they pitched them into the yard, and we stacked them up in the coal cellar, where for years they provided wonderful kindling. The roofers also tossed shingle nails around promiscuously here and there, and my bare feet received several punctures from them. We washed the places with yellow kitchen soap, and tied on the usual torn-up-old-sheet bandages, and fortunately, since they were house-roof and not barnyard nails, no harm was ever done. When we moved into the dilapidated house, my aunt Emma had sent Mother from Atlanta some rolls of new wallpaper to "freshen up" her bedroom and sitting room. We lived in the others as they were: no freshening for them. The bedroom paper was pink, striped and flowered, and after it was on, and with the sunshine pouring through the two long windows that went down to the floor, it was the loveliest room that I had ever seen, and I was proud to play and sleep there. For it was my room, too, as I had long ago taken Father's place in the big bed. From leftover pieces of wallpaper, for several years I made valentines, for the box at school, and others inscribed in a disguised hand, "To Mother, from Guess Who."

Beyond Mother's bedroom was an unfinished shed room, which took the place of an attic, and was my refuge from the boys' teasing. By the window in here was stored the old cradle, where I could double up (as I *had* to, for I was much too tall for it) and with a fairy book pretend I was a princess, an only child, with no hateful brothers.

The truth of the proverb "Other times, other customs" was certainly borne out by our kitchens in Oxford. They were large rooms, models of inefficiency and wasted space, with as many windows as possible, for "standing over a hot stove" was not just a figure of speech. A big iron range really heated up, and cooking went on all day long. There was always a cook in charge, and she never opened a cookbook. She scorned the kind of directions—such as "Level off a spoonful with a knife blade"—that were given in the new kitchen bible, *Fannie Farmer's Boston Cookbook*, which had just appeared. Oxford cooks never measured by spoon or by cup or any other contraption. They *knew* how much of an ingredient to use, and they threw in handfuls, pinches, dashes, and the results were mouth-watering.

The kitchens where they reigned were not scientific laboratories, but relaxed, sociable places with several splint-bottomed chairs, worn into pleasant grooves by much sitting in by cooks of comfortable proportions, and at least one chair would be a rocker. The black queen of the kitchen, on hand all day to watch over everything, sat a great deal of the time while she was watching, and often had a passing friend drop by and sit with her. The children in a family were also fond of hanging around in the kitchen, which was cozy and warm in the winter, and at any time there was the chance of there being something to sample, a bowl to be scraped, or a mixing spoon licked, or just to chatter with the cook and her friends, who were all their friends, too. Someone asked of a servantless house, "But who do the children talk to?" By keeping their ears open, children heard accounts of the exciting things that went on in Shakerag, the Negro section of town.

Our kitchen at the Griffin place was a typical one. Its central fixture was a great black iron wood-burning range. Once the fire got going, it furnished bounteous cooking space all over its top. The degree of heat depended upon how far a cooking vessel was placed from "the front of the stove," which was not really the front but the left side, where the fire burned. To slow something down, or just keep it warm, it was "put on the back of the stove"—i.e., the right side, away from the firebox.

It had a capacious oven, but no thermometer or timer. Recipes, which we both wrote and pronounced "receipts," read lackadaisically "bake in a hot oven until done," which wouldn't have helped a novice much, but made complete sense to all Oxford cooks, who were unnurtured on specific figures for degree of heat or length of time to leave in the oven.

Broiling was done by hand. Meat was slipped between two flat openwork plates of coiled wire, the fastening slide pulled down over the handles to hold it secure, and then the whole held over the open firebox, where the fire had previously been let to burn down to a good bed of coals. This was quite a matter-of-fact procedure, not thought to be at all troublesome; nor was the stove oven held responsible for its failure as a broiler. A statement in a 1903 cookbook said, "So near perfection have the makers of stoves and ranges come that it would be difficult to speak of possible improvements."

The prices of the steaks that these people broiled over the coals were

sirloin, 25 to 30 cents a pound;
porterhouse, 30 cents a pound;
round, 18 to 25 cents a pound.

The maw of a kitchen range was insatiable, calling constantly for fresh sacrifice, and in homes like ours where there was no regular manservant, keeping the kitchen woodbox filled was the children's never-ending job. Between it and the helter-skelter woodpile in our yard there were ten back-porch steps to be scaled, so bringing in armloads of wood was not a job that either of the boys were fond of. I much preferred reading fairy tales and pretending that I was a princess, not a household drudge.

An advertisement had recently appeared in newspapers and magazines for the newest invention, the Kalamazoo kitchen cabinet, which contained in a single piece of furniture everything needed in a kitchen: drawer space for pots and pans, a flour bin, shelves for spices and condiments, white enamel working space, wire racks for bread board and rolling pin. It was the last word in housekeeping efficiency, and a few of the more affluent Oxford homes owned the Kalamazoo marvel. As we were among the least affluent, there was no question of our raising our eyes to it; we got along quite comfortably with nails driven into the walls for pots and pans, and shelves put up by "Uncle" Frank Brown.

One fixture in our kitchen was Melissa Gardner, who was black, of course. Her official title was "cook," but she was such a poor hand at it that Mother, who had little talent in that direction either, had often to make things, following line by line the directions in that volume that had a place in every kitchen, *The White House Cookbook*.

There were a couple of big tables, one zinc-topped and one covered in oilcloth tacked under the edges. Melissa kept her dishwashing equipment on one—the bucket of water and bar of Octagon soap, and two large pans, one for washing, one for rinsing. Water came from the well and was heated in a big black iron kettle on the stove. The yellow soap, strong enough to kill germs when any of us had a cut or sting or stepped barefooted on a nail, was only for the kitchen; at the bedroom washstands we used Ivory, the white oval Fairy soap, or clear glycerin Pears soap. This last was advertised by the famous oil painting by Sir John Millais of a curly haired blond boy in a green velvet suit, blowing bubbles, and underneath was written, "Good morning, have you used Pears soap?" This was often said facetiously as a morning greeting.

For grease or ground-in dirt, Melissa used Sapolio, a cake of Bon Ami (which was advertised with a baby chicken and a slogan, "Like the chick that's newly hatched, Bon Ami has never scratched"), or a box of Gold Dust. (Its slogan was a pair of grinning little black boys who urged, "Let the Gold Dust twins do your work.")

Garbage was collected by an old black man, "Uncle" Bob Davis, who stumped around town all week from one kitchen to another, pushing a wheelbarrow full of buckets in which to collect slops for his pigs. Mother always had some food to give "Uncle" Bob for himself when he came around, but we licked our platters pretty clean ourselves, so there wasn't much left to give away, even to anybody as unchoosy as "Uncle" Bob.

There wasn't much throw-away-able trash. We followed the old early American slogan of "Use it up, wear it out, make it do, or do without." The paper things that fill wastebaskets now were not so plentiful. Any that were to be disposed of were crumpled up and used to start the stove and grate fires. In spite of the fact that letter postage was only two cents, there was no spate of direct mailing advertising, nor was there the plethora of organizations soliciting for dogs, cats, whales, wild horses, the halt, lame, and blind, conservation of this and that, and orphans of every race, creed, and color. We were in the happy condition of never seeing a letter addressed to Occupant or Resident. Congressmen and representatives on both the state and national levels left their constituents strictly alone. There were no paper towels, napkins, plates, sandwich bags, and drinking cups. We smoothed out any wrapping paper or bags that came into the house and kept them to use later, patiently untying knots in string and saving that, too.

There were few empty bottles or cans to dispose of. Canned vegetables or fruits were put up at home, and the same mason jars were used year after year with fresh rubber gaskets. No alcoholic beverages dared cross the town line, and soft drinks like Cherry Smash, sarsaparilla, or the new Coca-Cola (affectionately called for at a soda fountain as "a dope") were not bottled to take out. Kegs of these syrups were supplied to store fountains; the soda jerker squirted some into a glass and then filled it up with charged water—definitely something only for those with money to waste, and time in which to waste it while hanging around a soda fountain, i.e., college boys.

A standard part of every kitchen's equipment was the coffee grinder, for it was only in the whole bean that any of that beverage ever came in our doors. The rolling pin and a large breadboard were never put away, for there were hot biscuits made for three meals a day. On almost every kitchen table there was a contraption with a handle to turn, rather like a clothes wringer, for making beaten biscuits. These were for parties. There were the usual cooking pots and pans, kettle, waffle iron, pancake griddle, muffin and frying pans, Dutch oven, etc., all of heavy black iron, which worked well for the long, slow cooking to which they were subjected on the wood stove.

Many homes had recently acquired little ice chests, which were just that, zinc-lined wooden boxes intended primarily for the block of ice itself, around which milk and meat were tucked anywhere there was space. Cookbooks recommended, "If a home has no ice chest, milk, cream and butter should be kept in a cool, sweet room." All very well to say, but in hot summers, when the need was greatest, houses without ice chests were pretty apt to be without cool, sweet rooms, too.

Since drawing up water was such a chore, even the water that dripped into a pan under the ice chest was precious, and carried carefully as an offering to the many potted ferns everyone had indoors.

Ice was a problem for everyone. A horsedrawn wagon from the Atlantic Ice and Coal Company in Covington, peddling coal in winter and ice in summer, moseyed through Oxford twice a week, and its regular customers placed in a front window a diamond-shaped cardboard that said 10–20–30–50, turned the right way to indicate how much ice they required that day.

Following the ice wagon down the street was one of the joys of summer days. We trooped along behind it like the children of Hamelin Town following the Pied Piper. There was a step across the end of the open-ended wagon where the driver stood when he stabbed into the hundred-pound blocks to break off the quantity wanted. When he picked it up in his great tongs and carried it into the house, we rushed up on the step like a swarm of ants, and scrabbled for the chips and small slivers that had broken off. They were perfect for sucking. There were little splinters of wood in them and a queer woody taste. If they had too much dirt from the wagon floor for our far from fastidious tastes, we had only to hold them in our warm hands a minute, and the outside would melt and the dirt wash away.

If a family planned to have ice cream, a large extra block of ice was put in a galvanized tub on the back porch and covered with old newspapers and croker sacks until needed. Ice cream, the super and rare dessert, was always made at home in a churn packed around with ice chips and coarse ice-cream salt. It would be placed either on the back porch or in the yard, for as the ice chips melted, a stream of water flowed down the side, while a reluctant boy or man turned the freezer handle until the stiffened cream allowed it to turn no more.

The good-sized back porch onto which kitchens always opened was practically another room, for food preparation, such as shelling peas, picking chickens, etc., was done out there where it was cooler in the summer. There was a large ramshackle table where the lamp chimneys were washed each day. And above it there would be a long shelf or two, carrying among other things a row of clay flowerpots full of sand, in which cuttings were being rooted.

Underneath the shelves was an old nail keg that my brothers and I filled each autumn with little scaly bark hickory nuts. The nutmeats were encased in thick wooden shells, on which a regular nutcracker made no impression; a hammer and stone had to be used, but they were delicious and worth the trouble to pick out. Hickory trees grew in the streets, and the nuts could be picked up anywhere. Most houses, but not ours, had three or four pecan trees in the back yard, and occasionally someone had an old black walnut tree. Black walnuts were very special.

Off the kitchen was a pantry, of generous proportions, for flour and sugar were bought by the barrel, and many other things, too, in bulk that took up space. Although few houses had locks on outside doors, they all had locks on the pantry. This was necessary to prevent their contents from leaving at night with the cook to feed another household; taking food home with them was not considered dishonest by cooks.

The mistress of the house began each day by unlocking the pantry and "giving out" the ingredients necessary for that day's meals. In doing this, she must not be stingy-handed so that there was not plenty to go around (including what she knew would go home with the cook to feed her relatives waiting there for it), but she must also not measure out so lavishly that she robbed her own family.

A great deal of a family's food never passed through a store. Chickens, for instance, were snatched up, violently squawking, in one's own back yard, and had either their necks wrung or their heads cut off right there on the chopping block, then were plunged into a bucket of hot water, and feathers plucked off and insides pulled out—a horrible process, and if you thought about it at all, enough to turn you for life against eating chicken. But we didn't think about it. As a small girl I calmly watched chickens being killed both ways many a time, and then later ate a drumstick or a second joint with gusto.

Bread was never store-bought. There were always hot butter-milk and soda biscuits, round pans of egg-bread made with corn meal and cut in pie-shaped pieces, and loaves of light-bread made in each home. There was also the yeast with which to make it, a bit being always kept back to start the new batch. If we gave out, I was sent to borrow a necessary bit from a neighbor.

Eggs came out of our own hens' nests in the chicken house in the back yard. Each family was provided milk by its own cow. If there was none, or if she were temporarily dry, a neighbor's cow obliged, and someone went over with a pitcher. Pickles, preserves and jellies, catsup, chocolate sauce, and their like were all made at home, even though mayonnaise meant half a day of beating egg yolk and lemon juice with a fork, and adding olive oil drop by drop.

We ate prunes and dried peaches and apples, soaked overnight. An orange was a rare treat; sometimes the only ones all year would come in a Christmas stocking, to be jealously guarded from sib-lings. They were eaten by cutting a small hole carefully in the top with a pocketknife, through which to suck out the juice. Then we tore open the collapsed orange, and ate the drained pulp.

Any fresh fruits, berries, or vegetables came not from store bins but from our own gardens; blackberries and little wild plums and persimmons were picked in the fields by the children of a family. There was no such thing as having something out of season; we had to wait until things ripened. After being without them for a whole year, the first corn on the cob, English peas, or strawberries tasted almost too delicious for mortal eating.

3

"Our Little Village in the Grove"

When we moved to the Griffin place, I was six. It was right in the center of everything, where the post office, the Old Church, Palmer Institute, and the stores were, where just beyond the boys' tennis court, the mulecar went by with jingling bells four times a day to meet the trains.

And a lot was going on at our house, too. Not only were the jolly, friendly college boys who boarded with us coming in and out constantly (and often available to run under me in the tall rope swing they had made for me in one of the big oaks in front of the house), but ladies were always walking up to our porch at all hours and knocking. They came to talk to Mother about dresses, for now, with house payments to make, she had begun to take in sewing. She wasn't a regular dressmaker; she only "sewed for people."

I was old and responsible enough now to trot here and there downtown alone on errands, such as getting the mail. At first everybody I met asked me my name, but afterward, recognizing that I was a town citizen and belonged here, spoke to me and chatted. I carried shoes to the repair shop; I took notes to people's houses for Mother; I sometimes even delivered sewing.

Dr. Alexander Means, the most distinguished of Emory's early faculty, and the owner of the lovely old white-pillared house across from the post office, affectionately called Oxford "our little village in the grove," but to a six-year-old, it was the whole great wide wonderful world.

Although the Oxford founding fathers had banned business of any sort, they had soon found out that they had to let in a little. Where mules and horses were the means of transportation, there had to be a blacksmith's shop, and ours might have been ordered from Mr. Longfellow himself, for it fitted perfectly the lines of his poem. The smith, Mr. Thacker, was indeed a mighty man, with huge arms and chest, and his glowing forge with its flying sparks lit up the otherwise dark and mysterious interior of the shop. Besides the horse standing with one foot raised to be shod, and his owner standing by his head to quiet him, there were usually several idlers lounging around in the shadows, who found it a friendly place, with something going on to watch. I played with the blacksmith's two daughters, and one day when there was no horse waiting to be shod, their father made a ring for each of us by heating a bright new horseshoe nail red hot and bending it into a circle.

Although the smithy didn't quite stand "under a spreading chestnut tree," the only chestnut in town grew on the sidewalk just across from it. But we never got any of the nuts. The crabby old town carpenter lived just behind it, and watched each burr as it made up its mind to fall. By the time it was halfway to the ground, he was right there underneath, holding out his figurative pinafore. Harry and I always circled that way to school when chestnuts were ripe, but in all the years that we walked past, we never picked up a single one.

Mules and horses were not the only ones who had to have shoes renewed; after all the walking on the rough, unpaved streets, people did, too, so there must be a cobbler's shop. They also had to build a post office, for although situated out of the world, the little new mousetrap in the forest had a great many packages and letters, as well as students from all over the South, beating a path to its doors. And everybody certainly had to eat, and it couldn't always just be chickens and eggs and figs and peaches out of our own yards, so four tiny grocery stores had managed to edge their way in with necessary things like sugar and matches and lard. These stores were all within a stone's throw of each other, and constituted "downtown." None of them had signs, for everybody knew who owned them. The only printed sign in town said "Post Office, Oxford, Georgia"—totally unnecessary, but the government must have had a law about it.

This fascinating, pulsating world of "downtown" was only two blocks from the house where we now lived—one block this way, one block that—and it was not long before I had become a determined explorer. My older brothers were usually involved in their own concerns, and Mother was busy all day with housework and sewing, so I was often free to pursue my own affairs, and this frequently meant a meandering walk through the center of town. I would start at the post office, and from there go all the way down one side of the block that was the "business part of town," and after carefully looking to see that no wagons or buggies were coming, cross the car tracks, and come back up the other side. That way, I didn't miss anything. It might seem only a block's walk to some people, but to me, scuffing along slowly on the dusty sidewalk, or side-stepping mud puddles if it had rained recently, and stopping to pass the time of day with anyone I met with who would stop for me, it was an adventure.

There were five stores to check. None had big windows in front, but during good weather the doors were always wide open, and I could stand unobtrusively there, and give a good look around inside. In the same building with the post office was the first store, Mr. Henderson's, which had the best location, for after a man might pick up his mail, each day's unfailing errand, it was

Branham's Store

easier than not to pop in there for a can of Prince Albert or a plug of chewing tobacco. As a consequence, just outside was the best place in town to find the little tin tags that came on each plug, and which all the town children collected. Having no father at my house, I was dependent upon my bright eyes to pick them up in the dust of the sidewalks. I didn't do too badly, for living so near downtown I could make the rounds of the stores that sold tobacco more often than many children. Mr. Henderson's was the only place in town to buy seafood, and that only on Friday night. That afternoon the mulecar brought over a barrel of oysters that had come from Atlanta on the down train. In their house next door to the store, Mrs. Henderson fried them in crushed little oyster cracker crumbs, to be sold hot, four for a quarter.

Mr. Branham's store was next. His claim to fame was that when he was only fifteen, he had been the first Oxford boy to join the Confederate army, and he came home from Virginia with a game leg that made him lean on a cane for the rest of his life. He was usually sitting in a captain's chair near the doorway, the cane between his legs. There was no soda fountain in his store, so the students never went there. For that very reason, it was the one the faculty preferred, and they often stopped by for a chat with Mr. Branham. He had gone through college after he came home from the war, was what was called "a well-posted man," and could talk with the professors about almost anything. His store was as near to a club as they had.

If he wasn't there in the doorway, and no men were standing around, I used sometimes to go inside a little way and look for a few minutes through the front of the case that held several sorts of cheap candy. It was all jumbled together in a glass case "to prevent accidents," such as little fingers picking up a piece, if they had been out in the open. There was an inferior "bucket candy," judged good enough for children (and it tasted all right to me), long black licorice sticks, gum drops and lemon drops, orange-colored candy corn, and chewy pinkish-yellow candy bananas that took out many a first-grade loose tooth. (The alternative method was tying a string to the doorknob and then slamming the door.) Stick candy came in two flavors—peppermint with red stripes on it, like Mr. Rawlins's barber pole, and transparent lemon. There was also Crackerjack popcorn with a little prize in each box, hard ginger snaps called Zuzus, and animal crackers in a red cardboard box like a cage.

But I was more than a little afraid of Mr. Branham, since he was said to have killed several people in battle, so when he came back to the front of the store, I always sidled quietly out. There was doubtless no reason to be afraid of him; he certainly hadn't killed

The Tree That Owns Itself

anyone for years, and never little girls. Along with groceries, Branham's store carried fertilizers and stock feed at the back, and their queer smell filled the air. Several farmers' mules and wagons were almost always tied to the long hitching-rail out in front of the store.

All stores had these hitching-rails, as there had to be something to tie an animal to, and no one dared use a tree. For Oxford was very tree-conscious, realizing that the large ones were the town's greatest assets, and in laying out the streets and putting up buildings, the founding fathers had felled as few as possible. They also immediately set out along the new streets little water oaks to grow for a hundred years, and before the century was over, a town ordinance was passed to protect them all. It read, "If any person shall cut, trim, top, damage, or remove any shade tree from the sidewalks or streets of the town of Oxford, or hitch any horse, mule or any other beast to any of the same without written permission of the chairman of the street committee, such person shall be punished." And the town elders deeded to itself the finest of the original white oaks, then over eighty feet high, in order to be sure it escaped destruction at the hands of any later progress-mad citizens who might object to its location almost in the middle of the main street. "The tree that owns itself" is legally safe until time and old age claim it.

After Mr. Branham's store came the Stewarts'—not a store, but a big Victorian house where the Stewart girls, Miss Emmie and Miss Sallie, who were in their late sixties, ran a boarding house for students. Among others, all members of Phi Delta Theta, one of the top fraternities, ate there. Their little white clubhouse was just around the corner from the Stewarts', and before each meal Richard, Miss Emmie's head waiter, went out in the yard and rang a great dinner bell in their direction. Several years later, when waterworks were installed in the college gymnasium, Miss Emmie had them run a pipe up to the Stewart house, and she put in a white enamel bathtub—Oxford's first. Her friends of both sexes made appointments, like visits to the dentist, and openly carrying a large towel and a cake of soap, proudly told anyone they met, "I've been invited to Miss Emmie's to take a bath."

Next came the store called the Arcade, for the students. It carried their textbooks, athletic equipment, pennants, felt and satin sofa cushion covers for cozy-corners, stationery, and pin-up girls, which were drawings by Harrison Fisher and Howard Chandler Christy of girls' heads only, never shoulders or bodies or legs. It also had some large advertising cards with pictures of nattily dressed men in straw hats with stiff brims and pegtop trousers, from which suits could be ordered by mail.

I often came upon Harry hanging around outside the Arcade. He had made himself a shoeshine box, stocked it with polish, brushes, and old rags, and for a nickel he gave shines to the college boys, and this was the best place to catch them. He never liked for me to see him downtown, and would always tell me crossly to go straight home. And I would, only not *straight*, for this was where I crossed over and started back up the other side.

A really jolly store came first on this side, Mr. D. T. Stone's (no kin to us). A corrugated roof stretched over the sidewalk in front, with long plank seats between the posts, and there were benches against the store for loungers. This store was rather like an English pub, with checker games taking the place of a dart board; it was here that my older brother Lowrey, while still in short pants, became an expert player. Mr. Rawlins had a barber's chair in the back of the store, where the college boys got their hair cut.

Things were always happening at that store; it was a favorite with the students. Once when some Greeks came through town with a wagonload of bananas, there was a contest at Stone's store to see who could eat the largest number. Wagers were made, favorites backed, and, unknown to any of the faculty, who would have been scandalized, money changed hands. One of the college fraternities rented the whole floor over the store for their clubroom, and members were always going up the outside stairs to it, and sometimes you could hear a mandolin or a banjo being played there. Stone's had the first telephone in town, but since nobody else had one on which to call in orders, for a long while it was a poor investment.

Then came a stretch of several houses of people who really lived "downtown," even more in the heart of things than we did, but they were not anybody we knew well. The shoe repair man lived in one of them, and had the front room for his shop, with the uninviting smell of dust and old shoe leather. He was a grumpy old curmudgeon—at least, to me he always was, looking down his nose at the worn offerings I timidly held out to him, and growling that they really weren't worth another job, which would strike despair into my heart (what would Mother say when I told her?)—but he'd see what he could do. (Relief!) We were constant patrons, taking shoes to be half-soled for as long as they held together.

Although I never went over to investigate it, there was one more civic building besides the post office that helped make up downtown. This was a tiny calaboose standing at the end of a lane off the main street in a plot of overgrown weeds, made out of the stones left over from building the post office.

Oxford believed in preparedness, and if a crime wave ever did hit us, we were ready, not only with the calaboose in which to lock criminals up, but an appointed village constable to do it. But with no customers, he just stood around all day in a broad-brimmed black felt hat, a collar-button in his shirt band, chewing a wisp of grass. The only inmate the calaboose ever had was the Covington mason who constructed it. In celebration of its completion, before he arrived to put on the finishing touch, the lock, he had bought a bottle of whiskey in Covington, and by the time he had fastened the lock firmly in place, he was in quite a befuddled state. In trying out the lock, he inadvertently locked himself in, then passed out completely on the floor, and had to lie there until he sobered up enough to let himself out, which was not until the next morning. The constable never forgave him. It was his one chance of arresting a drunk, and all he could do was to peep at his unconscious self-incarcerated prisoner through the barred window.

The last store was the Johnson Brothers', situated under a magnificent water oak that in the summer shaded the benches in front. This store had the concession for Palmer's school books, which parents had to buy themselves, and tablets and pencils were usually purchased there, too. Its soda fountain will go down in history as having served the first Coca-Cola in the county, and almost the first outside Atlanta. This world-shaking event took place somewhere about 1895, before bottling, when ten-gallon and twenty-six-gallon barrels of the syrup were just beginning to be shipped to selected cities from its home base in Atlanta. Mr. Asa Candler, who owned the patent and made the drink, had a son at Emory, and he sent down a keg to Johnson's soda fountain as a treat for his son's college mates. When word got around that "the new soft drink" had arrived via the mulecar, the boys lined up for a quarter of a mile.

Coca-Cola's first ads proclaimed it "Delicious, refreshing, exhilarating. Very beneficial results obtained by its use in the winter months. May be served hot or cold." I never heard of anyone's drinking a steaming cup of it; the nearest to that was the Emory boys' way of dropping a nickel's worth of hot roasted peanuts in the glass.

It was a historic day when for the first time a drink of Coca-Cola slipped down the throat of an Emory student. Twenty or so years later, after Mr. Candler's gift of a million dollars, all raked in from the sale of this same drink, had effected the college's removal from Oxford to Atlanta, Emory was waggishly known as "the Coca-Cola school," and in 1979 this same drink made to the great university Emory had become the largest gift ever made to any college anywhere: one hundred and five million dollars. Johnson's store, as the place where Coca-Cola was first associated with Emory, would probably be pointed out to future generations.

Four grocery stores may seem quite a number for such a small town as Oxford, but their combined inventories did not add up to much; they were rather dull-looking places inside. A food store was not considered a proper place for ladies to go. Instead, a clerk made house calls around town to the store's regular customers, taking their orders, which were later delivered by wagon, or if the house was nearby, in a two-wheeled cart pushed by a big boy in a white apron.

Actually, what did they sell? Cans of kerosene, barrels of flour and corn meal and sugar, rice, grits, and "rat cheese" from a big wheel. On the shelves were boxes of baking soda and baking powder, salt and spices, vanilla and lemon extract, Walter Baker cocoa, Kellogg's cornflakes, ammonia, matches, soap, and lard. Sitting around on the floor were large cloth bags of black-eyed peas and dried peaches or prunes, to be scooped up and sold by the pound, their prices always staying at the same figures, written on a card and stuck in the mouth of the bag. The sight of the things in the stores was not really worth a trip downtown by a lady; except for the case of candy, there was nothing to lure even me inside.

Such, then, was the tree-embowered village of Oxford in the early years of this century—a college, a church, a grammar school, a post office and calaboose, a smithy, a cobbler's shop, five small stores, one with a barber's chair, and residences. In the seventy-five years since it was founded, there had probably been fewer changes than might be found anywhere else; little that was raucous had come to disturb its peace and beauty. It was still "a place set apart," with education the sole reason for its existence.

4

The Yellow Mulecar

Oxford was connected to the rest of the world by a little canary-yellow streetcar pulled by two mules, which four times every weekday made the round-trip straight across country to the nearest railroad station at Covington to meet the trains. Covington had one just like it, and together they constituted the C. and O. Street Railway Company. The fare was five cents.

Although the name Covington was a stop on the Georgia Railroad between Augusta and Atlanta, the town itself, a typical southern county seat, was a mile and a half away from its depot, with Oxford an equal distance in the opposite direction. At the place where the trains stopped there was nothing visible but a couple of cotton warehouses, and the mulecars, waiting on each side of the tracks.

The little car was a welcome, friendly sight to travelers returning to Oxford. Emory students coming back to college in the fall climbed aboard with delight. Everyone who rode it regarded it with affection.

Some progressive Covington merchants, wanting to get goods to their stores from the depot, had incorporated the little street railway company in 1873, but it was quite a giant step they were proposing, and fearing that they were engaging in too rash an undertaking, they had tremblingly thought it over for fifteen years before any actual work was begun. Covington citizens, however,

The Mule Car

especially the ladies, wanted a car not just to get to the depot, but to go on to Oxford as well. They liked to hear the visiting preachers, the numerous debates, glee club concerts, and other entertainments put on by the college during the winter. In June, Emory commencement was the social highlight of the year. Covington had the courthouse, and the litigation of the county, two small hotels, and a solid rank of one-story brick stores around the Confederate monument on the square, but for its cultural life it leaned heavily on its smaller sister town.

Once the first spadeful of dirt for the tracks was lifted, the air sizzled with excitement. Sidewalk superintendents really had something to watch now. The county weekly paper carried a blow-by-blow account of progress.

"March 13, 1888. Thirty-nine tons of steel rails, purchased in New York for $40.75 a ton, and three thousand crossties at fourteen cents apiece, are now being delivered on the line."

"April 24. We are now entering a new era! Still, we needn't get proud over the matter. It is just one of these modern improvements that come in our growth."

"July 10. The first car is a daisy! (It was purchased from the Orlando, Florida, street railway company.) It was placed on the tracks Saturday morning, and attracted unusual attention."

Indeed it had. It immediately ran off the tracks, and frightened half to death the people who had been daring enough to try the maiden ride.

The Covington line was completed first, and then in October the tracks were carried on to Oxford, where a barn was built at the end of the line, with room for the car and stalls for three mules—one always being rested. By the 1900–1910 era of which I am writing, it was an established institution; the gleaming steel rails down the main street were the backbone of the town, and the symbol of sylvan Oxford. Its deliberate pace fitted in well with the village's quiet, unhurried life. Youthful passengers would drop off and pick blackberries or sweet little wild plums along the way, and then hop back on again. The town's small boys used to "hook" rides, until the driver provided himself with a whiplash long enough for him to stand at his driver's post and flick bare legs crouching on the back platform out of sight. The sound of the mules' bells was a steady and cheerful part of our days; people without watches checked their schedules as the car passed. I considered myself lucky indeed to live where I did, for the tracks lay along the street that was on the side of our house, and I seldom missed watching the mulecar go by. Its passing through town was not only one of the sights; it was almost the only sight that moved.

Numerous tales were told of it through the years. A regular passenger was Colonel Ulla Hardeman, one of the few Oxford residents whose work was out of town. He was state treasurer, with his office in the capitol building in Atlanta, to which he went every day on the first up train. Departing early in the morning he was usually the only passenger in the mulecar, and he used to take advantage of this and save time by hanging up a little mirror and shaving on the way to the depot.

On one occasion, being late and not dressed when the jingle of bells and the driver's preconcerted whistle announced his chariot, in the dimness of early morning, Colonel Hardeman grabbed up an armful of what he took to be his clothes and rushed out in his bathrobe to finish dressing in the car. The car was late, too, that morning, and the driver started the mules off at top speed once the colonel was aboard. That gentleman discovered to his horror that he had taken not his own but his wife's clothes.

"Stop, stop!" he called frantically. "We have to go back!"

There was no turning around. The only way to reverse direction was for the driver to take the mules out, attach them to the other end, and head back toward Oxford. Having done so, they dashed as far as the Hardeman house, where this time the colonel made sure he brought along the right things. In the meantime, the mules had been again reversed, and never in their entire lives had those placid, slow-moving animals gone up Rivers Hill and to the depot in such a hurry. When they arrived, the panting train was standing there, ready to go, but the conductor, watch in hand, was giving his regular passenger a few minutes of grace.

Little courteous actions like this were possible then. Occasionally the Oxford driver was hailed by one of the Peed girls as he passed their house, and asked "to wait a few minutes, please, until Papa finishes a letter he wants to get off on the next train." The mules enjoyed the short rest, and the sky never once fell.

For the festivities of commencement week, a brass band always came down from Atlanta. When the musicians got aboard the Oxford mulecar, they would strike up a tune for a little sample of their wares, and the mules, unused to such a blast, almost always ran away. They didn't go very far with the heavy car hitched on behind, but every male shoulder among the passengers, no matter how exalted (bishops, for instance), had to be pressed into service to get the car back on the rails.

When the cars began to run in 1888, there were horsecars all over the country serving as regular city transportation, but long after electricity and trolley cars came to the cities, the Oxford and Covington mules were still slogging along. By the time we moved into the Griffin place the bright yellow of the first car had faded to a soft cream, and the grandchildren of the original mules, if mules could have had grandchildren, would have been pulling it.

On November 4, 1917, quietly, with no fanfare, the mulecars made their last trip. The Covington weekly newspaper, which had blared so blatantly for a whole year over their coming, gave their departure two lines:

"Covington, Oxford, the county, and the whole country bid a fond farewell to the old mulecars—now gone from us forever. 'Gone but not forgotten.'"

The *Atlanta Constitution* was kinder, devoting a farewell column on the editorial page, and publishing a picture that was captioned: "Last mule-drawn car in the country passes with the end of the famous Covington and Oxford line. It is estimated that if the mileage of their twenty-nine years of service were added up, the mules would have walked the equivalent of twice around the world." The tracks were torn up and became needed scrap metal. Mr. Nat Turner, a C. and O. Company stockholder, bought one of the old cars and parked it on his lawn as a playhouse for his children. Nobody can now be found who remembers what happened to the others. *Sic transit gloria mundi.*

5

The Other Grandmother

In order to be near my recently widowed mother and "be a comfort to poor, dear Ida," my mother's stepmother, also a widow, had moved to Oxford. A great many Methodist ministers' widows ended up here. She brought with her Mother's half sister Nell. I adored both Grandma Lowrey and my lively young aunt, just out of college, a vivacious belle around whom Emory students were buzzing constantly. Those who could afford it sent her long boxes that looked like corset boxes (corsets were about twenty-eight inches long) but contained something much different: they had come down on the train from Atlanta florists, and were full of long-stemmed American beauty roses. The offerings from my aunt's young admirers that I liked best, however, were the boxes of Nunnally's chocolates, occasionally even a mammoth box weighing five pounds.

Those were the days of the Gibson girl, and Aunt Nell was a stylish and lovely one, with a blond pompadour, saucy hats loaded with flowers and ribbons, long, swirling skirts, and petticoats with ruffles. Whenever she bought new shoes, vanity made her, like all young ladies, select them a little too snug, and mine was the delightful job of "breaking them in" for her, tottering around Grandma's rooms in high heels and delight.

They lived first in a little yellow Victorian cottage behind the Branham house, called Magnolia Cottage because of the two beautiful specimens of *Magnolia grandiflora* in the front yard. Grandma paid $2,000 for it—$100 down and monthly payments of $7. The price was low because a former owner had committed suicide there, and as a consequence it had been shunned and left vacant for some time. Oxford people were not superstitious, but even so no one wanted to live where such a thing had happened. Even Grandma, although she insisted that it made no difference to her, was rather relieved when she was offered the job as matron at the Hall, which carried a live-in apartment.

The Hall was a student boardinghouse, partially financed by the college. Here congregated the poorer boys, usually non-fraternity men either unable to afford fraternity expenses (some were missionaries' sons), too scornful of the snobbery involved to be willing to join one, or of such rural and unsophisticated backgrounds as caused them to be passed over in fraternity elections. They may have been poor in pocketbook, but they were far from it in brains. They often carried off the majority of college honors, and in later life became governors, congressmen, judges, and bishops.

The Hall was located across from the Griffin place on wide Fletcher Street, down which the car tracks ran, and since this grandmother was younger and more able to put up with children's noise than Grandmother Stone, I was a constant visitor. She was in actuality a quite spry old lady, but she always claimed to have some ailment or another—not enough to take her out of circulation and prevent her attending any gathering to which she wished to go, but enough to furnish a continuous topic of conversation. She delighted in dosing herself with a cure-all from a brown bottle labeled "Dr. Mosely's Lemon Elixir," and she took so much of it, and was so confident of its curative powers, that the Covington doctor described it to other patients as "Mrs. Lowrey's Lemon Elixir." Could Dr. Mosely's concoction possibly have contained alcohol? Perish the thought! Grandma was a devout member of the Women's Christian Temperance Union, as were all the other Oxford ladies who swore by Dr. Mosely, and she always wore her little white enamel ribbon membership pin on her shoulder.

The year that they moved to Oxford, the primary teacher at Palmer resigned to marry, and my aunt was asked to take over the class. I felt very important, being kin to one of the teachers! But an even more exciting thing happened in our family the next year: Grandma Lowrey announced that she was going to be married again. I couldn't believe it, for she seemed extremely ancient to me, and I had never before heard of a grandmother who got married. (She must have been only in her fifties.) But sprightly "Sister Lowrey," still in her widow's weeds, was a bride-elect!

My mother, whose idea of marriage was not only until death parted but through all eternity, had been stunned, too, when Grandma broke the news to her, but she had had several years of experiencing how desolate a woman's life could be without a husband. After leaving Oxford to teach in another town, Nell had married and settled there, and Grandma was alone as a boarding-house matron—not too glamorous an existence—so Mother was pleased that she would have companionship again, and move financially from being a widow living on a preacher's pension to the status of the wife of a small-town banker. And Mother had liked the jolly old man when he called at our house one day and facetiously asked Mother for Grandma's hand. When Oxford ladies heard what was in the offing, they said, "For pity's sake, Sister Lowrey!" Mother retorted with the equivalent of "More power to her!" This new husband, himself already three times a widower, had been one of my grandfather's friends. He was a sturdy, handsome, white-haired Confederate veteran.

On their bridal night, Grandma, dressed in her long white cotton nightgown, with a ruffle standing up around her neck and at the wrists of both long sleeves, with her prayers said, and her front hair decently done up in curl papers, was the first to climb into the big walnut double bed where three other brides had been before her. She then watched with amazement and horror as her seventy-four-year-old bridegroom slipped his suspenders down from his shoulders, stepped out of his trousers, unbuckled a stout webbed girdle around his waist, and *took off his right leg and stood it up against the wardrobe!* She knew, of course, that he limped, "the result of a war injury," but the dear soul had had no idea! It was too intimate a subject for an engaged couple to have discussed.

Although the marriage took her away from Oxford, it was to a town only three counties away, and she often came back in glory for a day's visit. For the new husband owned one of the new contraptions called an automobile, the first in his county and the first I ever saw, and he would drive in it from their home to ours at the highest rate of speed permitted by law and possible of attainment along the muddy, rutted roads—something like a vertiginous twenty miles an hour.

For the trip, he and Grandma both wore long straw-colored linen coats, called dusters. Mr. Mac had in addition a cap and goggles, and over a sailor hat Grandma tied a violet chiffon scarf, with long ends streaming in the breeze their rapid progress kicked up. When they descended on Oxford in this rig, I thought I had never seen anything so splendid. I hoped everyone in town was watching and saw them stop at our door. I needn't have worried; Oxford didn't have something like that happen every day.

It was nice to have the last memories of that good grandmother not as a staid "widder-woman" in black, unlocking the pantry at the Hall to give out an unexciting supper of grits and sausage for the boarders, but clutching a violet-scarf-streaming hat, beside a handsome husband on the front seat of a big automobile as she bounced into Oxford to dazzle the natives.

6

The Sage of Oxford

One of the town's best-known characters was my father's older brother, George, who never married but lived alone all his life, often the only inhabitant at the family home, the Thomas-Stone house.

As a boy of six, he had been blinded when a cousin's pet goat jerked a horn in one eye; the other eye later went out in what they called "sympathy," i.e., infection. But he had gone on with his life, even graduating from Emory, for his father paid the expenses of another student to room with him, take the same courses, and study aloud.

Now an elderly man, he still walked the well-known streets, aided by a long probing cane through which he knew every crossing. There were no rushing motor cars to threaten his safety, and everybody watched out for "Mr. George." Since he could not shave himself, a crisp beard had growth to a length of several inches, and with this, and his tall staff, flung out at arm's length with each step, he looked like a patriarch who had stepped from the pages of the Old Testament.

Perhaps no one ever loved every stick and stone of Oxford as he did, or knew them more intimately. He had served as mayor several times. He owned a small cotton plantation on the edge of town, and was his own overseer, keeping a careful figurative eye—it could not be an actual one—on everything. He walked between the rows and, by touching the plants, knew each crop's progress from planting to baling, carrying all the figures in his head until they could be entered for him in his farm record books.

He had a large hunting-case watch, with no crystal; by running his fingers gently over the figures, he could tell the time, and shortly after the mulecar had arrived each day with the Atlanta mail, he would appear at the cozy back room of the post office, and his friend the postmaster, after he had taken care of office duties, turned to Uncle George's secretarial work, reading him his mail and writing needed answers. He kept up a correspondence with several old Emory classmates; Bishop Warren Candler was one of them, and "Dear George" and "Dear Warren" letters frequently went back and forth, giving their several opinions on the Methodist Church's attitudes toward this and that. Uncle George preferred having his personal affairs taken care of this way, rather than letting members of the family know all about his business and offer advice. He neither needed nor wanted advice.

The postmaster read aloud the daily newspaper, and the two of them discussed what was happening in the world. Uncle George had no hesitation about letting elected representatives know just what he thought of how they were handling the citizens' affairs at both the state and national capitals. Occasionally, fired up by something that had displeased him in the way public affairs were being conducted, he would write a scathing letter to the Atlanta newspapers, which would appear on the editorial page with the heading "Another communication from the Sage of Oxford." He had an excellent mind, and from his position on the periphery of the rat race he often had a clear opinion well worth publication.

He was a regular attendant at Sunday morning church services, and once astounded the congregation by walking sedately down to his pew with his beard plaited in two pigtails tied with red

ribbon bows. I was the four-year-old culprit. It was while we were
living in the Thomas-Stone house with him, and that Sunday
morning, dressed for Sunday school and waiting for Mother to be
ready, I had climbed into Uncle George's lap out on the porch for
one of his famous stories. I often plaited his beard into two pigtails as I sat on his lap; a shake of his head would undo them. It
was just after Christmas, and Mother had given me two pieces of
red ribbon that she judged were too short to save and use again. I
had recently learned how to do that intricate thing, tie my shoe-
laces in a bowknot, and was very proud of being able to do it.
This morning, I decided to try out my new accomplishment and,
unbeknownst to Uncle George, tied two firm little red bows in
his plaited beard. At that minute, Mother called me, and I jumped
down and ran to her, completely forgetting the ribbons.

When he was a teenager, Uncle George had studied for a while
at the Georgia State Academy for the Blind at Macon, and while
there had learned to make brooms. He continued to carry this on
as a sideline to his farming, working in a little red cabin in the
back yard left over from slavery days. Here his clever fingers
turned out a light-weight creation of his own design, which he
called a "lady-broom." Servants preferred the heavy kind sold in
stores, but every lady in Oxford had one of Uncle George's lady-
brooms for her own use, and visitors to Oxford, enchanted with
their light weight and efficiency, sent orders back for them, so that
his lady-brooms swept homes in many towns other than Oxford,
and he was kept busy making them.

He was a famous teller-of-tales to the group of small nieces and
nephews who lived in his end of town. While he worked on his
brooms just inside the cabin's open door, we sat on the steps or
sprawled on the ground outside, entranced by his rendering of the
Uncle Remus tales, the Arabian nights, fairy stories, and especially

his reminiscences of things that had taken place right there in Oxford.

He had been a small boy during the Civil War, and remembered vividly things that had happened then, beginning with the day his father joined some neighbors cantering to the county seat to vote on secession. Sherman's path from Atlanta to the sea came right through Covington, and a group of his cavalry made a detour to see what excitement there was in Oxford. There was none until they arrived; then there was plenty. We listened to the tale of how the Yankees cleared out every pantry and smokehouse in town, took any jewelry or gewgaws that pleased them for their wives and sweethearts, and folded silk dresses and put them under their sweat-stained saddles.

Another of Uncle George's tales was of the Means home, which was Oxford's haunted house. He had grown up with Toby Means, who was supposed to be the "hant." When the time came for Toby to enter college, he balked, asking his father, who was the president of Emory then, to give him the money it would cost and let him go out in the world and build his life elsewhere, in his own way. But Dr. Means was a firm believer in as much formal education as one could get, and he refused. Toby, very upset and angry, in his turn refused to accept his father's decision as final, and kept nagging at him, hoping he would relent. Day after day, he would stamp back and forth on the long back porch to let the whole family know how angry he was over his father's attitude.

Then a little traveling dog-and-pony show came to Covington, and Tony was said to be smitten with the charms of a bespangled bareback rider. It was thought that he went away with the circus people, but no word was ever received from him, and he never came home again—except, of course, as this ghost, whose heavy tread was heard many times on the porch where he used to pace

The Haunted House

up and down. There were other unexplained things, too. Inside doors would swing open or closed when there was no breeze or draft, and a sighing could be heard in the halls and in certain rooms on perfectly calm days.

Years passed. The Means family dispersed and left Oxford, and other people bought the house. The footsteps and other mysterious manifestations continued. One such took place on a morning when the current owner was expecting a man to call very early to close a business deal. Before he was dressed, he heard loud footsteps on the porch, and thinking it was his client, he hurried to open the door. With his hand turning the knob, he still heard the footsteps. There was no one there.

The house was one of the loveliest in town, with spacious grounds, well kept up by each new owner, and was often chosen for commencement receptions, but no one seemed to want to live there very long. They all reported strange happenings, and Oxford, including Uncle George, firmly believed they were caused by the errant son, who, repenting his folly, had come home.

Uncle George could point out vacant lots where the houses that formerly stood there had gone up in flames. Since people in Oxford burned kerosene lamps, this was bound to happen every now and then at night, and there had been daytime fires too, innocently set by the owners themselves in the yard. There were no lovely stretches of lawn around the village houses, but grass of a sort grew at random in the shady yards under the big trees. At least, it did every spring, but by summer's end the sun and lack of watering had done for most of it. Whatever of the tough, dried brown grass was left was burned off in order to give the next spring's growth a chance. The idea was to choose a windless day, set the fire on the outer sides, and let it burn itself in toward the center. But no matter how dead calm the day was when the fire was set, striking a match seemed to be the signal for a breeze to spring up that fanned the flames the wrong way. Neighbors rushed to the scene. The flames were beaten out with old brooms, water would be frantically drawn up from the well, and bucket lines formed to move it from hand to hand. But once a house really was on fire, there was little hope.

Another tale was of the famous Kitty, a slave girl belonging to the wife of a bishop living in Oxford. The Church forbade a bishop's owning slaves, but Kitty refused to be set free and leave her beloved mistress. As a result, the Methodist Church had split into northern and southern segments in the years when the issue of slavery was dividing the nation. Kitty stirred up as much of a turmoil in her little puddle as Martin Luther once had in a larger Catholic one. Kitty had her way; she stayed with her white family until death, when she was buried in their lot in the Oxford cemetery—the only black person ever interred there.

There was a romantic story about the great bell that hung in Seney Hall Tower at the college and clanged out the hours. A Latin inscription, molded in the bell, told that it had been cast in a Spanish monastery in 1796, dedicated to the Virgin Mary, and it implored the holy mother to pray for the monks who had made it and for all the people in their little town who were within sound of its voice. It had been stolen from its monastery by the conquering Napoleon when he silenced all of Spain's bells and carried them to Paris to melt them down for French cannon. But for some reason this one did not meet that fate, and was thrown aside. (Perhaps the Spanish monastery had used inferior metal.) Years later, when he was taking the traditional "grand tour" of Europe in 1851, Dr. Means bought it for his little Georgia college. The monks and Spanish townspeople for whom the bell first interceded were long dead, but whenever we heard the hours strike on it now, Uncle George said we could know that it was still pleading to Heaven "for all the people within the sound of its voice."

Besides buying the bell and having a runaway ghost son, Dr. Means figured in many of Uncle George's tales. He was the most illustrious faculty member Emory had ever had. He had been a college president, teacher, physician, scientist, and inventor, always on the alert for new and strange experiments with which to astound Oxford. Emory students through the years, toiling in the science building over what they considered dull experiments, might well remember, and be inspired by remembering, that back in 1852, right here in quiet Oxford in his simple little laboratory, an Emory science teacher demonstrated what was probably the first incandescent light ever seen. (Edison's did not come until twenty-seven years later.) As the class blinked at the new light in amazement, Dr. Means prophesied, "Young gentlemen, this something which we call lightning, or electricity, is destined to become man's servant. The time will come when homes in the city of Atlanta will blaze at night with electric lights, and the cars will be propelled by it." There was no fanfare over the discovery. The students, unaware of its importance, thought of it only as something with which they might pad their weekly letters home, but if he had had a press agent, Alexander Means of Oxford might well have become a man known around the world.

Not everything that made Oxford an interesting and exciting place had happened in the long ago. Three eight-year-old girls of my own generation, inspired by stories in the Sunday school papers of children who had by hard work and perseverance gained money and "acclaim," decided to go and do likewise, sure that fame and fortune were waiting for them in Atlanta. They planned to run away there and make Oxford proud of them. With no money for train tickets, they would have to walk the forty miles. They set out, up the railroad tracks, pulling behind them a red express wagon with their supplies—a dress apiece, corn meal muffins, sausage cakes, gingerbread, and a fruit jar of water. But they didn't get far. Failure to show up for breakfast alerted one of the mothers, who hitched up the family buggy and rescued the runaways only minutes before the Augusta to Atlanta train came roaring on their heels up the track. It sounded like a glorious adventure, and being brought home after only three miles, and given a whipping to boot, was an unfair and inglorious ending.

Uncle George had had his own romance, and it continued, although he was alone now and blind. As a college student he had given an engagement ring to Emmie Stewart, "the prettiest girl in Oxford," but her family persuaded her not to marry a blind man, so the ring was returned. Neither of them married anyone else. After the Stewart family was broken up, Miss Emmie and her sister Sallie bought the big green house in the center of town, built by Dr. Dickey for his family and vacated when he became the college president, and ran a boardinghouse for students. Every Sunday night, through the years that followed, Uncle George went there for supper with Miss Emmie, and they spent the evening quietly together, usually she reading to him, while he held her hand, which again wore his ring.

7

The Daily Round

Neither locks had they to their doors, nor bars to their windows;
But their dwellings were open as day and the hearts of the owners;
There the richest was poor, and the poorest lived in abundance.
—Longfellow, *Evangeline*

It was a good thing that when the first town houses were built they had been given generous proportions, for it was not long before every inch was needed.

With very little money to run on, the college from the first was operated with Spartan simplicity, out of both principle and necessity. Buildings of classrooms and laboratories had been erected, but no dormitories. The original plan of housing students had been called "Helping Halls," cooperative groups of ten to fifteen boys who lived together, did their own housework, and raised vegetables and chickens in their back yards for food, at the cost of about nine dollars a month.

There was only one thing wrong with the plan: it didn't work. The unsupervised living arrangements offered "too numerous facilities for mischief and disorder." Faculty and townspeople might be pious and placid, but college boys were evidently neither, and were constantly demonstrating that they were far from being docile and submissive young saints.

A typical prank had been leading old Pompey, the Latin professor's horse, in the dead of night up the stairs of the main college building, where his bewildered whinny from a second-story window greeted the faculty and students when they arrived for morning prayers. The high jinks and rowdiness went on all the time, and the frazzled mentors had to abandon the Helping Halls plan.

The solution seemed to be for the faculty to take the boys to live in their own homes, where they could have stricter supervision and their high spirits might not soar so high. This was voted on at a faculty meeting, and the professors then had to go home and confront their wives with the news.

In a small town, with nothing going on, it was rather a welcome note of gaiety to have college boys come to live. In scholarly Oxford, where people looked down their noses at all commercial transactions, it was not called "taking boarders," but "having a few boys." Most homes were large, and one or two rooms could easily be spared for them, and with two boys to each double bed, the small student body was promptly stowed away. The "Stewart girls," Miss Lynn Branham, and Mrs. J. Z. Johnson took so many that they turned their big homes into regular boardinghouses. Miss Lynn fed forty in her basement dining room—those who lived in her house and boys who roomed in nearby homes which did not furnish meals. And there was also the Hall, where my grandmother Lowrey was matron for several years.

Oxford's black population provided plenty of help—knowledgeable cooks and waiters, and always young scullions hanging around the back doors, only too willing to make themselves useful. The problem facing the good ladies who ran these dining halls was not servants, but *ice* during the warm months.

Cold weather brought other worries. There was no central heating, and the winters were far from tropical. Shivering citizens would tell each other that their thermometers registered "two below," or even occasionally "six below." (Of course this didn't mean below zero, but below freezing.) Coal-burning grates did their feeble best to heat drafty rooms, and keeping coal scuttles filled, as well as kindling on hand, and hauling out ashes were constant tasks all winter long. Morning bedroom fires were seldom built. A cold room hurried the dressing process, or family members could gather up an armful of clothes and carry them to where a fire was already built. But at night, oh, those icy sheets!

Building a fire in a cold grate and then keeping it going was quite a chore. Beside each fireplace was a "blower"—a tin shield to hold over the fireplace opening until the draft got really going. And on each mantelpiece was a vase of spills—slender twisted rolls of strips of newspaper used to transfer a light from the grate to a lamp or a man's pipe. (They saved matches, and a bunch of spills was a useful thing for a little girl to make for her mother or aunts as a Christmas present.) The winter greeting to a visitor was "Come over to the fire!"—and people spread out their cold hands to it, and backed themselves up to it, and propped their feet on little hassocks made of bits of carpet remnants to keep them off the cold floors.

Houses were lit by kerosene lamps, and at night the little town would have been blotted out completely if it had not been for their soft glow shining out of house windows. Although people usually spent the evenings after supper at home, they made a few excursions along the dark streets, such as to Wednesday and Sunday evening prayer meetings, and on these occasions a lantern swung from a hand. A source of illumination gratefully made use of whenever possible was moonlight. An almanac giving the changes of the moon lay on each parlor table, and was consulted whenever dates were set for future evening jollifications. Full-moon nights were the most popular, of course.

There was no shoveling of snow to contend with, but good red Georgia mud more than made up for it. The dust that in dry weather rose in gentle clouds whenever a team of horses passed along the unpaved streets had a magic power of turning into the muddiest of muds. On one end of a porch step was affixed an iron foot scraper, and people made sure to use it before entering a house in wet weather. "Go back and wipe your feet!" was automatically called by mothers to small sons.

There were no window screens, and in warm weather, with no fear of tramps or thievery, the front door was always left hospitably open. All you had to do was walk in and call out for whomever it was you had come to see. Black people always went to the side or back doors, where they also "just walked in."

In hot weather, guests were greeted with "Won't you have a glass of fresh water?" and a member of the family was dispatched to draw up a bucket from the well on the back porch or in the yard, drawn cold enough from the depths of the earth to frost a glass.

An unbelievable amount of water was required in a home's daily routine, and it was all hoisted up bucketful by bucketful from the well with a windlass. The only source for hot water was the kettle on the kitchen stove. No wonder the Saturday night bath was enough for most people. Children who had gone barefoot all day had to have a pan foot wash at bedtime. At our house, drawing the water was theoretically the boys' job, but when the cook needed some and the bucket was empty and the boys were not yet back home, she often had to fetch it, and so did Mother.

On a washstand in every bedroom there was a big china bowl and a pitcher to be kept full, a slop-jar on the floor beside it to be kept emptied, and, discreetly out of sight in a closed compartment at the bottom, a matching chamber pot. The clang that its top made when put back on was unmistakable, like no other sound in the world, and distinctly audible in the next room. Ladies usually tied little crocheted caps on them in an effort to deaden the sound. Lamps had to be kept filled, their smoked chimneys washed daily.

Seeing to all these things needed to keep a house running—warmth, light, water—consumed an inordinate amount of time every day. Other things took time, too. To get a message to anyone in town, a note had to be written and dispatched by a child or servant, if one was handy, and a reply waited for. Out-of-town plans had to be made by mail well in advance, allowing plenty of time for answers. Since people rarely traveled to see each other, in lieu of talk sessions long letters passed between the feminine members of the family, telling all the news. Dr. Moore's wife, who had two married daughters in distant states, and a great many other out-of-town relatives and friends, set aside one day a week for her correspondence, letting it be known that on Thursdays she neither made nor received calls or transacted any other business but her personal letter-writing. It seemed a good idea, and several other faculty wives adopted it.

Students boarding in a household enjoyed not only the privileges of family life, but the restrictions as well. Every evening, in every family in Oxford (except ours), they were expected for family prayers in the parlor. After the reading of a Bible chapter, everyone knelt before his chair, eyes closed, rears pointed toward the center of the room, while a prayer of thankfulness was said for the blessings of the day, followed by an entreaty for protection through the coming night. And the prayer was always answered, too, for no one in Oxford had ever "died before he waked."

Each morning they remained at the breakfast table until another Bible chapter was read, and a protecting prayer offered before going out to encounter Oxford's pitfalls and dangers. These latter were not overwhelming.

The reason our home held no such observance was not that we were a godless, atheist crew, but simply that since Father's death there was no male head of the house. Mother had been brought up in a minister-father's house, where all matters were regarded in their relation to religion, but it was a *man* who did the dealing with God. No woman could presume to such leadership as that of praying aloud in a group that included men. (In a small circle of ladies at a missionary society, it was permissible.) And Mother still dutifully held to "what Papa had thought."

She was a timid person, anyway. Who was she, that she should feel herself capable of addressing the Creator of the Universe out loud, before a roomful of college boys? No, never. Bedtime children's prayer conducted at her knee, repeating the prescribed "Now I lay me," was the only contact with the Almighty that she felt her unworthy self capable of handling. Her boarders found no fault with this omission of lengthy daily family prayers, nor did we; we would have been overcome with embarrassment to hear our mother talking to *God* out in front of other people.

Whenever I spent the night at another little girl's home, and the next morning her father commended me to God by name before everybody, for safekeeping during the day, I was too embarrassed to meet anyone's eyes when the long prayer at the breakfast table was ended, and I hoped that God would understand that it was none of *my* doing.

At our fatherless house, Mother made do by blessing our food before each meal with the briefest grace—"Give us grateful hearts for these and all Thy blessings"—murmured almost shyly, by praying nightly in her room that none of us die before waking, and by attending with her brood thousands of church services. Surely, she hoped, this would be sufficient to slip us through the pearly gates when the time came.

8

Always on Sunday

Sunday really began on Saturday night, for that was when the Sunday-best clothes were laid out and inspected to be sure everything was in order. It was then that the aroma of shoe polish arose from every back porch in the village, as shoes (for many besides us, the only pair) that had scuffed around in the dusty streets all week were brushed and burnished and made fit to bear their owners into the House of the Lord.

The church was the center of Oxford life, and the Sunday school the department that especially catered to the children. We all went, of course, just as we all went to Palmer Institute on weekdays. There was no separate building for Sunday school; it met in the church. Two closed rooms up behind the pulpit were used for the primary and infant classes, and the rest of us were scattered around in small groups throughout the main body of the building, in sight but supposedly out of hearing, yet near enough for boys and girls in separate classes to signal surreptitiously to each other and spell out messages on their fingers. We learned this finger alphabet almost as quickly as the one in the school book.

The Sunday school suggested the reading for the younger generation by means of a small lending library of moral books, and every Sunday, "papers" were given out in the classes, which along with the explanation of the next Sunday's lesson for study included a short story. It was always about worthy children who, after sticking it out through unbelievably tough experiences, reaped a glorious reward. We liked stories like this—trials, but glory in the end—and swallowed them whole. They were about a world different from ours. We read, envied, sighed, and then tried to resign ourselves to our own uneventful lives.

After Sunday school, which came first, most children were required by their parents to stay for the preaching service. It was not as much fun, of course, as Sunday school. If you were very young, it was quite all right to stretch out on the seat with your head in your mother's lap and go to sleep, but for older children it could be a very long hour. There weren't many things to do other than following through the hymnbook the messages written by an earlier bored child: "If my sweetheart's name you wish to see, look on page 53," and on 53, "You must search some more: look on page 74," and so on and on. You never did find out who the sweetheart was, but looking for it helped pass the time.

From church, it was home to Sunday dinner, which was the meal-of-the-week, with "the big pot in the little one." Entire families of relatives were invited to other relatives' homes almost every Sunday; often a second table was necessary for the children.

Two Sunday afternoons a month were given over to two children's organizations, and most of the town children belonged to both. The Helping Hands (or what we called the "Heppin' Hans") was the name of the Children's Missionary Society, that distributor of mite boxes, which took the place of piggy banks. Oxford was very mission-minded, especially with regard to foreign missions. Mother was in charge of it—the equivalent of a den mother.

At the Heppin' Hans meetings in our sitting room, the children sat on chairs to the extent they were available—dining room chairs were brought in, too, of course—or else cross-legged on the floor. Someone from the Women's Missionary Society told us or read us about the heathen in Africa and the Far East. The only things that stuck in my mind, after lasting through years of this, were that in India a wife had to drink her husband's bath water, and be burned alive if he died first, and that in China they flung most of the girl babies at birth into some sort of pit and let them die. Those that didn't get flung had their feet bound, so they could only totter around when they were grown women. This meant they were aristocrats and had to have servants to wait on them, since they couldn't walk around to get anything for themselves.

We sang about India's coral strand, warbled "'Come over and help us,' they cry," and took up a collection, for each child had brought along a few pennies tied up in a corner of a handkerchief. Then came the best part, for after a prayer the meeting was over, and we burst out of the house like an explosion and played in our big yard for about an hour before everyone had to go home. Games like tap on the back or kick the can, for so many children and with as many grand places to hide as there were around our yard, were a lot of fun. One afternoon some of the smart-aleck boys hid in the men's privy. Of course, the girl who was It couldn't go there to look for them, so she had to give up, and when they swaggered triumphantly out, home free, we girls were righteously incensed. From that time on, before we started to play, we announced, "No fair hiding in houses of any description," which always brought sniggers from the boys.

When the Heppin' Hans met, a Sunday afternoon around our house was not as completely noiseless a day as the neighbors might have wished, for whooping and hollering were absolutely necessary for a game of hiding, and Mother accepted this and did not attempt the impossible job of disciplining a yardful of children. The heathen had pretty well exhausted her by that time.

The other children's organization was the L.T.L. (Loyal Temperance Legion), the junior department of the W.C.T.U. (Women's Christian Temperance Union), which hoped to keep us from the demon rum forever by catching us young and telling us about the havoc it was wreaking everywhere in the world but Oxford. On joining, we had "taken the pledge," and each meeting began with our rising, lifting our right hands, and solemnly repeating it:

> I promise not to buy, sell, drink, or give
> Alcoholic liquors while I live.
> From all tobacco I'll abstain,
> And never take God's name in vain.

We had some dandy songs, with the words made up at the National W.C.T.U. headquarters, to be sung to familiar tunes. One started off "List to the tread of many feet" and wound up with the shout, "*Saloons, saloons, saloons must go!*"

Another, which we yelped out with vigor, was about animals:

> Now, whoever heard of a poor old horse
> That had to go reeling home,
> Because he had taken a drop too much
> Of somebody's poisoned rum?

There was a verse about a dog that abstained from strong drink, and another about a cat that was a teetotaler, too, and the last verse tied it all together:

> So when we are great big grown-up folks
> And while we are children small,
> We'll have as much sense as the dogs and cats
> Or we will not drink at all.

While the Oxford white citizens were as good as gold and proud of their liquorless town, not all of the Negro men always toed the line, nor did all the college boys. Some of the wildest of the latter used sometimes to buy the stuff in Covington and get hilariously drunk. The college faculty had plenty of discipline

The Outhouse

problems with these young men. But we children knew nothing of this; we repeated the pledge once a month at our L.T.L. meetings, and gave the good ladies in charge cause to hope that our generation would grow up to be exemplary citizens.

When the Heppin' Hans wild Indians were not running all over the yard, and only her own offspring were present to keep in line, Mother had definite rules about what could or could not be done on Sunday afternoons. It was all right to read, to look at pictures, to cut out paper dolls, or to paste in scrapbooks. I could play with my dolls, but not sew for them. As I figured it out, doing things with paper was all right, but with cloth was wicked. A threaded needle meant eternal damnation.

On most Sunday afternoons, my mother, my two brothers, and I filed dutifully up the hill to call on my grandmother Stone, and leave a respectful kiss on her soft, wrinkled ninety-year-old cheek.

Oxford citizens felt that Sunday afternoon walks out to our two "sights"—the Waterfall and the Rock—were perfectly acceptable excursions for the day. The Waterfall, where a husky little stream poured down gray rocks, was about a mile and a half out of town. In the spring, wild pink and orange honeysuckle, yellow jasmine, bird's-foot violets, and sweet shrub were scattered through the woods around it, and if you stood in exactly the right place, you could hear an echo. We asked the appropriate question, "Who are you?" and the echo gave back the regular answer, "Youuuu."

To get to what we called the Rock, a mile and a half farther on, it was necessary to cross over the Waterfall, not a dangerous leap at all for long legs, but rather stretchy and even scary for those that were not so long. The Rock was wild, moorland-looking, uneven ground, with broad outcroppings of gray granite, and with reindeer moss and other orange and crisp gray mosses growing in little pockets of soil here and there. Stone Mountain, the largest solid rock in the world, was only ten miles or so distant, and small patches of the granite occurred all along this land. (A nearby town was so stony that it was named Lithonia, from the Greek word for *stone, lithos*.) This section, unfit for cultivation, had been left in its original wild state, and was a great place for picnics. It was barren enough for a campfire not to be dangerous, big enough for a party to break up and spread out into small groups, or to go off on solitary excursions, perhaps stretch out for a nap with a hat brim tilted down over a face, and yet small enough for nobody to get lost, and for everyone to be easily assembled again for a picnic meal and the trip home.

Professor Bonnell, who lived at the lower end of Oxford and loved a Sunday afternoon walk, would often start from his house with field glasses, a knapsack in which to bring home any treasures found, and for company whichever of his children or the Peed girls across the street who wanted to come along. As they made their way through town, any other children or grown-ups who felt so inclined joined them, so that by the time he got to the

Waterfall, Professor Bonnell often had quite a number strung out behind him.

When they reached the woods, staffs were cut for walking sticks, and in the spring he made whistles for the children from lithe twigs whose bark slipped around easily. A child always came back from these walks with a treasure or two: a smooth white rock to add to the narcissus bowl, sweet shrub buds crushed in the corner of a handkerchief, a wild violet plant scrabbled out by the roots and rammed, dirt and all, down into a pocket, to put in the flower beds. And on the walk home at the end of a happy but tiring afternoon, there was not the sudden remembrance of homework for tomorrow's classes still to be done to rise up and ruin everything. Instead, we had the week's holiday of Monday to look forward to. School was closed on Monday, for doing homework on Sunday was sinful.

Mother had told us of a New England family of children, the Beechers, who were never allowed to play on Sunday until the day was quite over, and the signal for that was three stars in the sky. As dusk came on, these disciplined children used to sit quietly on the porch steps, scanning the heavens for the third star. When it popped out, a great shout arose, and they rushed off to play some game. Sunday twilight often found me sitting on the front steps, too, exhausted after all the day's activity, pretending I was one of the little Beechers, and watching for the third star.

9

Village Goings-on

Admittedly, Oxford was not a wildly exciting place, especially for students who came from sophisticated city homes, but to those of us who had seldom been beyond Covington, it seemed a buzzing community. Somehow, between education and religion, the days were filled. Although one of the students once wrote home, "After the leaves have fallen in the autumn, nothing moves here," there was always something going on.

Sundays were especially full, with three religious meetings at the church (and nothing short of being sick in bed was an excuse for not attending)—Sunday school, eleven o'clock preaching, and prayer meeting in the evening. Between these last two, students often sandwiched in a walk alone in the woods to practice aloud the coming week's assignments in oratory or debating, which were popular courses. Or they might have the Covington livery stable send over a rig to take a young lady buggy riding. There was one great objection to this: at some point before the ride was over, the horse was sure to relieve himself vigorously right in front of their four eyes—a very embarrassing moment for young people. So a young lady might often refuse an engagement for a ride, and prefer a long walk. (A plan to go somewhere in the company of the opposite sex was called an "engagement," never a "date." Dates were something like 1066 and 1492.)

On weekdays, daylight hours were taken up with classes, and for the students, with athletics as well. They had several tennis courts, unenclosed, but with backstops, and a rudely laid-out athletic field for football, circled by a running track. The small red brick gymnasium had traveling rings, a leather vaulting horse, space for marching, an area for exercises with dumbbells or Indian clubs, and a marked-off basketball court. There was no swimming pool; this was before the days when everyone learned to swim as a matter of course.

The faculty kept fit not by doing anything very strenuous, but by walking to classes, Sunday afternoon country rambles, and exercising a few minutes on rising every morning at the open window with a pair of wooden dumbbells. Faculty wives felt they were getting plenty of exercise when they walked around in their yards, cutting flowers for the vases, or—after the yardman had hitched up—when they drove around in their buggies in the afternoons to pay calls, to shop in the Covington stores, or simply to "take the air." The main thing prescribed for good health was "getting out more"—breathing Oxford's pure, unpolluted air, and not any form of exertion when once outside. The children's little arms and legs began exercising and pumping fresh air into their lungs the minute they woke up in the morning.

All evenings were peaceful. With no streetlights, there was no inducement to stumble around in the dark. People took cover.

How *did* people fill the hours?

The "glorious business of education" took care of most of them, for the evenings were given to study. Children did homework around the big lamp on the dining room table, and then joined Mama and Papa in the parlor for reading aloud. There was all of Dickens to go through, and if they finished him, Sir Walter Scott was waiting in the wings. They sang around the piano—hymns, serenades, folk songs; there was chess and checkers, and as many as four could play a hot game of Parcheesi. They talked to each other; parents dealt out advice to their offspring.

College boys put on isinglass eyeshades and bent over their books on the little study tables in their bedrooms. Or they strolled, whistling, over to their club rooms for discussion of this or that with their fraternity brothers, to strum guitars or banjos, sing together, or play chess or checkers. A great deal of masculine whistling went on, especially by anyone walking or working alone. Each fraternity had its own shrill whistles, both a call and an answer, and the members used them constantly to signal each other; a piercing whistle would reach far on Oxford's quiet streets. At glee club concerts, after the words of several verses of a song had been sung, another would almost always be whistled through.

To pass a pleasant evening after the next day's assignments had been completed, the romantically minded often sat in porch swings with local young ladies, who prepared for the engagement by making a plate of fudge or divinity candy. If it was a warm evening, the boy would draw up a bucketful of fresh cold water from the well, while the young lady rolled and squeezed lemons for a pitcher of lemonade. And sometimes, on Saturday nights, the whole town "cut loose" with affairs that were purely social, with no educational or religious strings tied to them. It might be a magic lantern show in the Old Church or the Alkahest Lyceum circuit show, which made an annual appearance with a fifty-cent admission program, and was worth every penny. There were no half dollars lying loose around our house, so we had to take other people's word for this. The write-up in the Covington paper said of one such evening: "The audience was kept practically in an uproar, either laughing at the humor, or on the point of tears at the pathetic. The program consisted of dialect readings, songs, a few pieces for the violin, and a collection of jokes hard to beat."

We were not dependent entirely on the space offered by the Old Church, for when sliding doors were pushed back into the walls and the whole downstairs "thrown together," many Oxford homes were large enough to take care of receptions and programs. Nor did we have to wait until out-of-town professional entertainers arrived to furnish amusements. We had talent of our own, and there was no charge to hear them.

Elocution was the great thing just then, with two schools of delivery, the Delsarte method and the Emerson method, and several of our young ladies had had correspondence courses in one or the other and were proficient in giving "readings" with gestures. So along with the never-absent piano selections an entertainment would also have a "reading." Sometimes the two would be combined: the words of a poem recited to piano chords at just about the same fashionable step-halt, step-halt tempo at which wedding attendants came down the aisle. Not every lady had the presence to be a good "reader," but all had been raised under the same rule of daily compulsory practice, and by dedicated pounding during their growing-up years, every one of them was a more or less competent pianist. They were a great addition to the local cultural life, never evading a performance by "not having brought my music," for they all knew several things by heart, and were delighted to oblige, adjusting the piano stool to the correct height by a series of twirls, laying a little lace-bordered handkerchief at the end of the keyboard, and then plunging into one of their pieces from a recent copy of *Etude*.

After the Meltons came to Emory from Johns Hopkins, things were much more lively. Professor Melton and his Baltimore family stirred things up considerably and brought a breath of city air and sophistication into our village life. Mrs. Melton was horrified to learn that the missionary society was the town's only women's organization, and she immediately started a "cultural group" called the K.K.K., after one she had belonged to in Baltimore. It meant Kil Kare Klub—no relation to the Ku Klux Klan. It met in rotation in the members' homes once a month, with a "paper" written with much agony by some member, followed by chicken salad and beaten biscuits and coffee, and then erudite discussion provoked by the paper's topic. The ladies adjudged sufficiently intellectual and socially qualified to belong to this group were definitely perked up by it all; the missionary society meetings came in a poor second.

Oxford ladies did not always have their eyes on culture and improvement. In the afternoons they were sometimes frivolous enough for a few tables of Rook, with a prize for the highest score and a booby one for the lowest—something ridiculously funny that was supposed to salve the feelings of the afternoon's poorest player. Rook wasn't a very complicated card game, and little girls would play it too, but we preferred Flinch, while we sat cross-legged on the floor of the porch or the cool hall. "Spotted cards" was what we called regular playing cards, which were so wicked that they were never seen in Oxford. An Oxford lady once certainly proved her total ignorance of them by saying innocently, "Why, I wouldn't know an ace from a spade!" Liquor, dancing, and gambling were outlawed by the charter, sternly forbidden ever to cross the town line, and as we understood it, playing with "spotted cards" was what was meant by gambling.

Once one of these nefarious items was discovered caught in some leaves on the Palmer girls' playground. We gathered fearfully around to look at it from a safe distance. Emphatically we did not want it to continue to pollute the place, yet none of us was daring enough to pick it up to dispose of it. (There might be blue jays around, who would report us to the Bad Man.) A bold soul finally got the fire tongs from the schoolhouse and with them carried it at arm's length and popped it in the stove. A sanctimonious little procession of girls who had followed to see the deserved fiery end breathed a sigh of relief that it was off our playground!

Having a college of several hundred young men meant that they quite often provided our entertainments. The Emory glee club gave concerts throughout the year, even rumbling off in a big two-horse wagon to perform in nearby county towns. (A far cry from days to come, when the glee club from Emory in Atlanta would travel by jet to European and South American capitals for its concerts.) The college had two literary societies, Few and Phi Gamma, passionate rivals, which often put on a lively debate about questions of the day, or presented an evening of orations to which all Oxford and Covington flocked.

The town's young people and the college students frequently had evening parties. If the occasion was specified as "formal," the students wore their Sunday blue serge suits; if it was a "tacky party," everybody looked around for the worst old, disreputable garments they could lay their hands on, trying to look like tramps, and perhaps joyously letting down the bars on proper behavior. But at all parties, even candy pullings—and the young folks had these, too—there were always plenty of keen-eyed chaperons. Besides going on picnics at the Waterfall and the Rock, students sallied out into the countryside on hayrides. Driving around on rutted country roads in a springless farm wagon may not sound like much fun, but under a full moon, with hay cushioning the ride and all the prettiest faculty daughters tucked in, a jaunt of this sort could provide a very enjoyable evening.

In a college town, of course, commencement week was the social high point of the year, to which everything led. There were goings-on in every home. Chickens fled for their lives, but were remorselessly transformed into pulley-bones and drumsticks. The handles of ice-cream freezers were turned all day long on back porches. There was icing of cakes and whipping up of elegant desserts.

Oxford had no hotel. Commencement week was the only time when we were flooded with guests, and we felt about it the way Robert Toombs did when a hotel was suggested for his hometown of Washington, Georgia: "There is no need. If a stranger is a gentleman, he can stay at my house, and if he isn't a gentleman, then we don't want him in town!"

So, in lieu of a hotel, every Oxford house was gaily crowded to capacity with out-of-town guests—parents of students, nostalgic alumni, trustees, dignitaries of church and state who were the "speakers," and pretty sisters and sweethearts in long swirling skirts and lacy, flower-trimmed hats, carrying ruffled pink parasols. For an entire week no child slept in a bed; several quilts folded together made a pallet on the floor, and we were only too proud to give up our beds for important company.

Commencement was a kind of social, intellectual, and religious Chautauqua. There were sermons every day by noted preachers, long programs of orations by the best speakers in each class, and conducted tours of the library-museum and science laboratory (which had a skeleton on display). There were also athletic events to watch, both outdoors and in. A relay race had panting runners "passing on the message"; on the gym floor, boys—wearing what looked to me like their summer underwear—marched around and around in intricate formations, swung from one end of the building to the other on traveling rings, and leaped up on each other's shoulders and formed human pyramids to a breathtaking height.

Evening was the time for the glee club to shine, and for parties given by the various Greek letter fraternities, which outdid themselves to entertain the visiting belles. The culmination of these was the Pan-Hellenic reception. With no dancing allowed, these eve-

ning affairs were formal receptions and prom parties, largely conversation, with couples walking up and down and with a constant
change of partners. Girls had little fancy prom cards with tasseled
pencils swinging from them, and each young man saw to it that
the young lady he escorted had a partner for each promenade. At
the tinkling of a little silver bell, a new partner would present
himself. Inside the house, crowded with people and brightly lit by
dozens of candelabra, behavior must be decorous, but when the
promenaders strolled along the dim walks and driveways of the
yard, there was opportunity for less proper and more satisfactory
flirting. The grounds were illumined for the occasion by Chinese
paper lanterns; the house chosen in which to give the party usually
had twisting walks and driveways on which to pace, and garden
benches and little latticed summer houses.

At each end of the long veranda would be a cut-glass punch
bowl brimming with a non-alcoholic punch, whose chief ingredient was strong tea. Each fraternity had a list of little girls from the
town, faculty daughters or younger sisters of members, who
served at the punch bowls, wearing their best white dresses, with
a pale blue or pink sash and a whopping matching hair-ribbon
bow on top of their heads, large enough to lift a girl right off the
floor. No sixteen- or eighteen-year-old visiting belle went through
more thrills and chills over the correctness of her costume for
these evenings than did the little ten-year-old servers of punch. At
the end of the evening, there was always ice cream and cake.

After commencement, the college boys went home, and at first
the town seemed empty and forlorn. But many things filled the
long summer vacation. The year I was eleven, the minister's
daughter and I (she was that indispensable thing in a little girl's
life, my "best friend") filled it by reading through the entire Bible.
The way we happened to get involved in this enormous undertaking was that our Sunday school teacher offered a crocheted purse

(very stylish just then—the directions had been printed in the *Ladies' Home Journal*) to any girl who would read the Bible all the way through. Neither Mary nor I had ever had a purse of any sort, having nothing to put in one, but some day we should, and this was a chance to get it free. And since it wasn't a tense competition, with only the first one through a winner, and since the long summer stretched ahead with nothing else to do, we decided to try. We did most of the reading, chapter after chapter, sitting in Mary's family's buggy in their side yard, its shafts on the ground. At first the unfamiliar Middle Eastern names seemed an insurmountable hurdle, until I had the brilliant idea of skipping all the words that began with a capital, unless it was an easy one we already knew, like Cain or Moses. (Mary always insisted that she thought of it; well, it doesn't matter which of us did.) It saved ever so much time, but even at that, it took us a whole summer.

The summers were visiting time for children. To provide a change and a treat, most of them would be sent off on the train to stay with relatives in another town. Two weeks was the regular length of such a visit. But when the nieces and nephews and grandchildren of Emory faculty, sent by parents to benefit from our good water and pure air, came to visit in Oxford, they stayed all summer. A number of them came every year, and both they and we felt that they were almost as much Oxford children as we were.

Summer was also the time for picnics and for watermelon cutting on the joggling boards in the yard. When the moon was full, the whole town brought a picnic supper down to the deserted college grounds and had a mammoth party, with the children shrieking and tearing around in the moonlight and playing games on the campus, where ordinarily we were forbidden to go.

Each summer there was the annual Sunday school picnic, when we piled in wagons and drove a long way off, not just to the Rock or the Waterfall but perhaps even to the banks of the Yellow River.

Parents went along—at least mothers did, and a few fathers were there to drive. Great hampers of food were carried—stuffed eggs, cheese straws, fried chicken, gingerbread, sliced ham and beaten biscuits, layer cake, tea cakes . . . We stuffed ourselves, went wading, and played games—kissing games, too, like "many, many stars," since there were boys along.

In late summer came cotton-picking parties. Cotton picking was considered Negroes' work, and the races did not trespass on each other's labor preserves. No matter how hard up an Oxford white person might be, he simply did not go into a cotton field as a "hand." The only time one could pick cotton was with a group, as a lark, and to give the money raised to some good cause. During all the time when we needed money so badly, it never occurred to Mother or either of the boys, or to anybody else, to suggest that they could make a little money by picking cotton. It wouldn't have been much, but something. Even when the soles of our shoes were worn through—and they could have made forty cents for every hundred pounds picked in fields within walking distance—it simply never entered anyone's head. But every fall, when the cotton fields were white, a Sunday school class or the children's missionary society en masse, carrying big cloth sacks, would get together and rumble out to a field in the country in somebody's father's wagon—the regular mode of mass transportation before buses. There we would divide into teams and spend the afternoon each trying to beat the others in number of pounds picked. It was hard, hot work, but fun. Then back to ice cream and cake at somebody's house, and on the next Sunday the number of pounds picked and the names of the winning team would be announced to the whole Sunday school, when a check for the amount earned was made out for a mission school in China, or whatever the chosen charity happened to be. And the little Oxford pickers, some barefooted of necessity, and some wearing cut-out cardboard soles to block the holes in their worn-out shoes, beamed with pure delight, and never once thought that it might have been more sensible to have let the charity begin at home and outfitted *us* with decent footgear, since cold weather and school were just around the corner.

Except for commencement, fall was the most exciting time of the year in the village. The hot, dusty summer had come to an end. The city children who always came to spend the vacation with relatives here had been bade goodbye until next year, and put on the train for home. The sweet gum trees were purple and red, the tulip poplars and hickories a soft yellow, and the giant oaks a dignified bronze. The days were crisp and sparkling with the herbal fragrance of goldenrod and ripening broom sedge everywhere, and with each arriving mulecar and its load of new college students, the haunting, long-held notes of the cry "New bo-oy!" from the throats of the old ones floated through the air.

Not only the college, but Palmer Institute too was flexing its younger muscles for the term coming up. There might be a new teacher to take the measure of; hems of school dresses had been let out (and horrors, a line there often showed it, too); boys with pocketknives were under requisition to whittle points on new pencils; and at Johnson's store there were lovely new varnished pencil boxes, with roses painted on a sliding lid, which tore your heart out.

The new college year was beginning, and all Oxford was "up and at 'em" with renewed vim. The town's houses were turned upside down for the fall cleaning, which put spring cleaning completely in the shade.

Mattresses and pillows had already been dragged out on a sunny porch, or lacking such, all the way into the yard, and given a thorough airing. A stiff feather dipped in turpentine was run along each mattress seam "just as a preventative." A needed lick of paint was put on here and there, and fresh putty pressed around window panes to keep out drafts and rattles. Everybody was getting ready for the boarders.

Cold weather brought no ice and snow, so there were no so-called winter sports, but now was the time for fun indoors, such as candy pulls, when a pot of molasses taffy was boiled on the stove at the school or in someone's kitchen.

In the week before Christmas, the same Sunday school class that had picked cotton for the heathen in September bundled up and, sitting close to keep warm in a nest of hay in a wagon body, made a nippy, nose-freezing trip out into the country to take collected food—jars of their mothers' canned vegetables or preserves—to "poor folks." (We did not realize that *we* were "poor folks.")

As for Christmas itself, a boy in the family climbed an oak tree and hacked off a bunch of mistletoe to hang in a doorway to "catch" people under. We cut sprays from the holly and other evergreen shrubs in our yards to take to the cemetery and to decorate the house. On Christmas Eve we also celebrated with fireworks, just as on the Fourth of July. We thought setting off firecrackers (bang! bang! Christ is born! bang!) was quite the proper way to usher in the blessed day. The louder the bangs in the daytime, and the more we lit up the sky at night with sparklers and roman candles, the better. An evening of fireworks made a glorious celebration because with no streetlights there was pitch-blackness for a background. I was afraid of all of them, except sparklers and the very small "squib" firecrackers that came in a batch of about a hundred, with their tiny wicks woven together. I would unravel these, and set off only one at a time, and then be frantic after I had applied the match, for fear that I couldn't throw it before it exploded in my hand.

The boys would boldly light the whole mass of firecrackers together, toss the batch in the air, and enjoy a peppering of pops.

They also had big giant ones that made as much noise as a small cannon—in fact, they were called "cannon crackers."

Each year the newspapers carried stories of children in other places who were maimed by fireworks, but since nothing so violent happened in Oxford, we went right on with our noisy celebration.

On Christmas Eve Mother read us the story from Saint Luke, and also the hilarious chapters about the little Ruggleses in *The Birds' Christmas Carol* by Kate Douglas Wiggin. The next morning there were the stockings with a coin in the toe. Some children had gold pieces; for us it was always a shiny dime, and one year, an especially hard one for Mother, just a gleaming Indian head penny. The long stocking-legs were filled with goodies from the box that two of Father's old friends in Macon faithfully sent each Christmas. There were apples, scratchy raisin clusters full of seeds, all sorts of nuts seen nowhere else all year—almonds, nigger-toes (Brazil nuts), English walnuts—and those wonderful treats, *oranges*! The box always had a bag of "bucket candy" for us children and a box of lovely chocolates for Mother. Each of us had a present for the others, usually things we had made ourselves and kept in the greatest secrecy, and there were always the Octagon soap wrappers to fall back on.

The only Christmas tree in town was a stout pine put up in the Old Church for the Sunday school. In the big bare building, lit by real candles, it was a beautiful sight. It was just as well that there weren't trees in private homes, or there would be fewer of these houses left, for the little tin holders, clipped on the branch ends, and swaying and tipping, always held the lighted candles at every possible dangerous angle. Buckets of water were lined up against the wall, just in case, and men and boys stood by ready to use them. Happily they never had to.

Everybody in town came. A woman played the piano, and we

The Old Church

sang Christmas hymns and the old carols. The minister read again the passages from the New Testament telling the Christmas story—the shepherds, the wise men, the stable, the star. We knew them by heart from previous years, but liked to hear them again.

Then families lighted their kerosene lanterns and walked home together along the dark, unpaved streets.

10

Palmer Institute

Not long after we moved to the Griffin place, the schoolhouse door swung open for me. There would have been only eighty-seven pupils at Palmer if *I* hadn't rounded it off at eighty-eight.

Before the town was even incorporated a primary school had been started. In 1860 the stately building of Palmer Institute was erected and became at once, next to the church and the college, the center of the town's life. Everybody had a stake in it; there was only one home in all of Oxford that had no children. All my Stone uncles and aunts and my father had been pupils here. For several years it had been sprinkled with first cousins and my brothers. Now it was my turn. Mother stitched up for me the regulation double gingham schoolbag to be carried half and half over the shoulder, with a slit in the middle to insert books, and I was off on the great adventure.

With four teachers, Palmer carried children from the first grade through the tenth, and did such a fine job (it had good material to work with—no sows' ears we!) that its graduates went immediately into the sub-freshman year at college.

The primary teacher seldom lasted very long. She was usually a pretty young thing just out of college, and by Christmas had been engaged off and on to at least four of the Emory seniors. Over the summer she married one of them, and the next September, there was a new face at the primary teacher's desk.

From Tuesday morning until Saturday noon the town's whole younger generation was gathered here, buzzing as busily as a hive of bees. Monday was the holiday, for Oxford was a strict Sabbath-keeper, and there must be no temptation to do homework on Sunday.

All the children came on foot; to go to the trouble of hitching up the family buggy to deliver able-bodied children somewhere was ridiculous. What else did children have to do but get to and from school? For those who lived in town, the chattering gang walk to school, with additions all along the way, was almost as much fun as recess. A few who lived out on farms had several miles to walk, but neither parents nor children considered this a hardship, for a child's principal job in life during these years was getting an education. If a wagon passed, they got a ride, but wagons were few in number and the trip was usually done slogging along on foot the whole way. If it meant a three-mile walk, a three-mile walk it was.

We town children tried to finish up our Kellogg's cornflakes or Sunny Jim or Force breakfast food and get to school early enough to have some time to play before the principal came out on the front steps and rang the big bell. We played what we pleased and how we pleased. No teacher ever supervised the yard, either then or at recess. Teachers were hired to teach us things we did not know; we knew how to play. There was no playground equipment, for our own arms and legs were all we needed. When baseball was in season, boys brought their own equipment from home.

The schoolyard was stark and bare. There were trees, but no attempt was made at beautification with shrubbery or other plantings. What went on *inside* the building was what was important, not how it looked from the street. One side of the yard was for the girls, one for the boys. On our side, we organized giant steps, drop the handkerchief, guinea-guinea squat, statue, stealing steps,

Palmer Institute

pretty girls' town, go in and out the windows, hold up the gates, pussy wants a corner. With a stick, we drew the squares for hopscotch. In the spring we turned rope for a line of girls to jump. Baseball was exclusively male, as were leap frog, wrestling, crack the whip, horseshoes, and red rover. (Touch football and frisbee hadn't been invented.) Fox and hounds was one of the few games that boys and girls played together, the more participants the merrier.

The practical reason for the division of the playgrounds was the separate privies at opposite corners of the yard, set far over on the back edge. Each was a regular three-holer, along with a fourth small one for the younger children so they wouldn't get wedged in. Outside the girls' privy was a honey locust tree, which dropped its long, sweet brown pods when they were ripe. A trip there ended with gathering as many as would fit inside a blouse without too obvious a bulge, to take back inside the schoolroom and bite into when the opportunity offered, or to trade to the boys, who had no locust tree. We liked the sweet, sickish taste.

For a visit to the privies during school hours—"having to be excused," we called it—there was a signaling system: you waved a finger frantically in the air at the teacher; one finger for what was delicately known as "number one," and two fingers for the more serious business of "number two." Also, one finger raised in the air but not waved frantically meant you would perish if you could not go to the water bucket for a drink.

There was no well at the school; the trustees were afraid that a child might fall in. Each morning designated bigger boys went over to Mr. Rufe Meadows's well close by and drew a bucketful for each room. We drank from a tin dipper, and then put it back in the bucket, heeltaps and all. On the bench with the water bucket was an enamel pan in which hands could be washed if they really got too bad—we weren't overly particular—or a nosebleed cleaned up. Above it hung a roller towel, changed occasionally.

These were the years before Kleenex. The teachers kept small torn squares of old, worn-out sheets in a desk drawer, and doled them out when mothers, who also tore up their old sheets for the same purpose, had neglected to supply their drippy young ones. When girls got into the middle grades, and wanted pretty handkerchiefs, more for show than for blow, they rolled the edges of little lawn squares between forefinger and thumb (first moistened with spit), and whipped on lace. "Stealing" these was the goal of each enterprising boy. A girl who didn't get her handkerchiefs stolen was a social failure; the boy who stole most efficiently was regarded with admiration as quite a "ladies' man." By the time my oldest cousin Tom was ready to leave Palmer, he had accumulated so many girls' handkerchiefs that his mother sewed them together and made curtains for his bedroom.

All desks were for two pupils, and except in the primary room each desk had a hole in the middle in which to wedge an ink bottle. There was a groove on each side for pencils. The lady teachers wore their pencils stuck through the topknots of their hair. There were no pencil sharpeners; points were made with a pocketknife, and a great deal of time was consumed at school every day in taking care of this. Every boy except the littlest ones carried a knife. It was a necessity, and not only for pencils; a boy must be able to whittle, to make himself a slingshot, and do with it many other things a boy had to do. If he didn't already have a knife, it headed the list of things he wanted for Christmas.

In each room there was a stove, and being nearer or farther from it on cold days made a considerable difference.

The school did not take children before their sixth birthday, although six-year-olds were often shifted immediately into the second grade, as I was, for in those faculty homes where reading aloud was the usual family evening entertainment it would have been difficult for a child to keep from learning to read by the age of six, or even five.

No lunches were served at Palmer, either hot or cold. (A *kitchen* in a schoolhouse? School was for education, not cooking.) We brought lunch from home each day in a round tin pail, and what we ate at recess had to hold us for the rest of the school day. There might be an apple, a hard-boiled egg, and biscuits with a slice of ham or flat sausage cake inside. A baked sweet potato was a good thing to take, cold by recess time and enough to tie little stomachs up in hard knots, but apparently it never did. Tea cakes, sugar cakes, or ginger cakes were good lunch-pail dessert treats. If we wanted a drink with our meal, we went to the bucket at the side of the room and scooped a dipperful of water. The school provided no milk.

We might have sandwiches made out of peanuts (which we

called goobers). *The White House Cookbook* told us how to make them: "For peanut sandwiches (very healthful!), roll parched peanuts and put them between slices of light bread, spread thickly with butter." Another favorite was butter-and-sugar sandwiches. Soft butter was spread thickly on slices of light bread, then sprinkled with as much sugar as would stay on.

One's first day at school is always a memorable occasion. At last, to belong. No longer to be left forlornly at home while every other child in town flocked to Palmer. I went in such joyful anticipation, prepared to believe my teacher an angel from heaven, and found there an unfeeling fiend, and the most horrible experience of my life thus far.

Desks were double, and were assigned alphabetically and by sex: two girls, two boys. I was at the end of the first-grade roll, and when my name was reached, no other little girl was left for a seatmate. But there was one little boy left, also an S, and—may the good Lord forgive Miss Hayes for doing it, for *I* never shall— she assigned us to sit at that double desk *together*.

My deskmate was even more horrified than I was, looking forward to what he would have to suffer at recess from the other boys. The lucky wights whose names began with B and F and L were delighted; a wave of giggles swept the primary room. The doomed couple sat each as near the outside edge as it was possible to do without falling off into the aisle. We laid our brown rat-tailed penny pencils in the pencil groove. I spit on a corner of my handkerchief and rubbed the top of my side of the desk—accepted procedure for primary housekeeping.

I was blind with tears of humiliation. I could never face anyone again; I could never even go home. As soon as school was out, I must run away, as far as I could go, and forever. I only hoped that Mother's life would not be ruined, too, that people in town would not make fun of her for having a daughter *who sat with a boy*! There was no question of any further education for me, for of course I could never show my face again in that schoolroom. But of course I did, and somehow survived. Since I was already a glib reader for a six-year-old, I was moved up to the second grade almost at once, and given a seatmate of the right sex.

On the very first day of school the next year, an important thing happened. When each new pupil rose to give his name and age, we were electrified by this pair of remarkable statements from two Branham grandchildren, who had just come to Oxford to live:

> "Martha Branham, eight years old."
> "Virlyn Branham, half an hour later."

Twins! I had heard of them, but never seen any. A child with two heads, or a centaur, could not have seemed more wonderful. To my surprise they looked just like the rest of us; the differences must be under their clothes where they didn't show.

In the third grade, ink bottles came into our lives. There was a hole in the top of each desk, where a bottle wedged in was supposed to be stable, but accidents did happen. We were also furnished with the concomitants—a penstaff with a fitted metal point, a blotter (constantly in requisition after each juicy new dip into the bottle), and a little square of cotton flannel with which to dry the metal tip when writing class was over. In my joy at arriving at this exalted state, I produced my first poetic effort:

> I love to think
> I love to think
> That now at last
> I write with ink.

The September after that, a fourth-grader now, I moved into the big middle room. There was a recitation bench, formerly a church pew, and the class scheduled to be next under fire would file over to it. Reading, writing, grammar, history, geography, spelling, arithmetic—we had a busy schedule. It was most important that we learn to write a clear, legible hand because, we were told, it was often the deciding factor in examination papers or for employment later. So now we began grappling with "copy books."

First we "warmed up" (wrist loose!) with a line or two of connected O's whirling into each other. This was the Palmer method, named for the man who had the idea, not for our school. We then filled entire pages with painstaking copies of the precept written at the top of each page in round, beautiful script:

> Strike while the iron is hot.
> Always do your best.
> Christmas is coming.
> Do good deeds.
> Pretty is as pretty does.

In geography, when we got to maps, we did not merely color black and white ones, already printed, into a yellow France and a pink Italy and a green Germany; instead, first we drew the outlines of countries, measuring off blank sheets of paper in squares with numbers across the top and letters down the sides to guide our outlines. We zigzagged in rivers and made ranges of mountains with rows of carets. Only then did we begin coloring in the countries.

History questions were never the easy true-false ones, with a fifty-fifty chance of getting it right, no matter how little you knew, such as "T or F: Fort Ticonderoga is in New York." Ours were fiendishly phrased like this: *"Where* is Fort Ticonderoga?" We diverted ourselves in history class by devoting time and talent to decorating the pictured faces of our country's great leaders. They were all given beards, mustaches, and spectacles, and General Sherman was in addition accorded horns and a long tail, twisting down the margin of the page and ending in a prong.

We diagrammed sentences as long as the chalk supply held out. Half the class would go to the blackboard, and each took a sentence from the grammar and made a great gangling skeleton of it. Then the other half, one by one, with a pointer explained what had been done, and parsed. We struggled with irregular verbs, and wondered how the English language got to be the way it was. (If it was *sink, sank, sunk,* then why not *think, thank, thunk?*)

In arithmetic there were the tables to be chanted: "Tootums six is twelve, tootums seven is foteen." It was a relief to get to those blessedly easy five and ten times-ses, which even the smallest child already knew from playing *hiding*, where you counted to five hundred by one or the other. Even the elevenses were nice up through ninety-nine; after that it became difficult. Multiplication, addition, subtraction, long and short division we *had* to master, for they were all done with pencil and paper, with no mechanical aids.

We learned to spell not by plunging blindly at a whole word, but by painstakingly working it out syllable by syllable: C-o-n Con, s-t-a-n stan, Constan, t-i ti, Constanti, n-o no, Constantino, p-l-e ple, Constantinople. Who could ever forget it after that? It was too bad we so seldom had occasion to use the word.

We lined up for spelling, toeing a certain crack in the floor, and the successful speller "went ahead" of the person who missed the word.

> I'm sorry I spelled the word,
> I hate to go above you . . .

Schedule and *rhythm* were terrors upon which many a good speller was wrecked. There were spelling matches within grades, and with the best spellers of the other schools in the county.

English, French, mathematics, Latin, and history were subjects that the big boys and girls studied. On the completion of the tenth grade, the girls "put up their hair," had a trunkful of new dresses made, and went off to college, usually to Wesleyan in Macon. The boys had less fuss made about them, for instead of the excitement of going off anywhere on the train, they simply walked down to the other end of town and became Emory students.

Although we applied ourselves ever so diligently, Palmer was not all work and no play. Saturday was Speech Day, when each of us, from the first grade up, had a chance to perform before the whole school. An educated person was expected to be able to speak well in public, and the Saturday recitations helped eliminate stage fright and instill poise. We learned quantities of poems and orations that stayed with us for the rest of our lives. The boys— not the girls—competed in county oratoricals held annually in the Covington courthouse. "The public is invited," the county weekly newspaper had advertised, "whose sympathy, good wishes, and prayers are asked." Large crowds came, their buggies and wagons filling all the hitching space around the square. The prizes were five-, ten-, and twenty-dollar gold pieces, and the Nobel prize simply wasn't in it with the fame that winning one of these brought. Names, and sometimes even pictures, were printed in the county newspaper. A gold piece was a favorite thing to give as a prize.

Throughout the year, there were jollifications. In February, a valentine box in each room caused excitement, and we labored over handmade offerings for it, drawing purple-petaled violets with long curving stems, hearts traced around a cardboard pattern, pierced with an arrow, and with drops of blood falling out.

> If you love me like I love you
> No knife can cut our love in two.

Such verses were written hundreds of times. There were also store-bought "comic" valentines—printed in color on a sheet of cheap paper, with an exaggerated cartoon of a person with a large head, eyes, ears, teeth, and a rude comment on how smart or pretty the victim mistakenly thought he or she was. "Teacher" was the main butt of these cartoons. They were often downright cruel, making fun of a limp or false teeth or some other deficiency. These were especially popular with the older, rougher boys.

In cold weather we had candy pulls for which tickets were sold at ten cents each. A kettle of molasses taffy was boiled on the flat top of a schoolroom stove, and with buttered and floured fingers we pulled away with a will until our dollop could be manipulated no more. Another special time was Arbor Day on a June Friday, when we dressed up and planted a tree on the school grounds for our descendants.

The older classes had spirited debates. "Resolved, that the cow is more useful than the horse"; "Resolved, that the steamboat is more useful than the railroad train"; "Resolved, that girls should not play basketball." (*Girls* play basketball? Don't be absurd!) But a few weeks later this item appeared in the Oxford news column in the county paper: "The girls at Palmer Institute have just purchased a splendid basketball outfit, and are making plans to learn the game."

With several grades present in one room, the teacher couldn't always be watching behavior in other classes while she was hearing one class recite, and Palmer children did not always keep their eyes fixed on hard work and the goal of a good education. Pinches might be given, or kisses stolen in the cloakroom. Property was never deliberately damaged, except for initials carved on a desktop. Pocketknives were for sharpening pencils, and for whittling, not weapons; a broken school window was always an accident committed with a baseball, never done on purpose with a rock.

But spitballs were made and thrown, and ends of pigtails or curls dipped quietly into an open ink bottle. The big blue Fry's geography book held erect did its best to protect a crouched culprit, but it could not hide everything. The boys boasted to the girls that they smoked in their privy "rabbit tobacco" (the withered leaves of the weed called life everlasting), but of course we never knew.

On April Fool's Day, it was the custom for the little boys to run off at recess, and some of the bigger boys had to be dispatched to bring them back. Once, as the afternoon had advanced, and no bigger boys had appeared, the truants began to feel uneasy, and to speculate as to what their punishment next day would be. One piped up comfortingly, "Well, they dassent to kill us!"

Being kept in either at recess or after school was a rather common occurrence for both boys and girls, but not anything to be proud of—quite the contrary. A penance that wasn't bad, if someone you liked was sharing it, was to be made to "beat 'rasers," that monotonous clop-clop behind the building where you were enveloped in a cloud of chalky dust that whitened your clothes and hair and dried your hands and made them look like a spook's.

Sometimes a boy, or even once in a blue moon a girl, might be slapped, when a teacher's patience had been tried to the limit. And a whipping was given occasionally to a boy if the offense was considered really heinous; but this was a last resort, and seldom done.

For over half a century old Palmer reared up in its red brick dignity on its bare, tree-shaded grounds. Every child who ever went there loved it, and there was universal mourning among its far-scattered alumni when one winter night during 1910 a stove fire was carelessly banked and the building burned down. The new school, an undistinguished structure chock-full of modern conveniences, and looking just like every other school in ten thousand towns, could never replace it in our hearts.

Perhaps more practice in reasoning things out for ourselves, and working out solutions to situations, would have been better training for our minds than all the memorizing we were set to do. But adults in charge of education then did not feel that grammar school children were mature and wise enough to suggest to the world how it should be run. They were convinced that learning by heart "the best that has been thought and said in the past" was the way to train young minds to produce worthwhile ideas of their own. During that early age memorizing is easy, and I have never regretted a single thing I stored away then. Many a time I have defeated insomnia by repeating to myself the soporific lines that begin

> This is the forest primeval,
> The murmuring pines and the hemlocks
> Bearded with moss, and in garments green . . .

And the gentle words of "Thanatopsis" have often in adult life

> . . . stolen away my sadness
> E'er I was aware.

II

That Old-time Religion

.

In Palmer Institute's primary room I had begun at the age of six to contribute my small bit to furthering one of the purposes for which the town had been founded—education. At nine I saw my name added to the list of those laboring for the second—religion.

The place where it happened was the New Church, for the town's first house of worship, a starkly beautiful and white frame building built in 1842, had just been relegated to being the Old Church, and there was now, Heaven forgive us, the New Church. A large structure in the beaux-arts style, it was completely out of place in a little village like Oxford, and was made of that regrettable material, yellow brick, with colored glass windows, Corinthian columns at the entrance set high at the top of a pompous flight of wide stone steps, and, as a crowning bit of pretentious architecture, a dome. The college had put it up, and owned the building, but the town was allowed to use it for its many religious services. We did so with pride.

Congregational singing had a large part in all such services. Led by a choir of "young people" seated high behind the pulpit and with their legs and laps modestly hidden by a short brown velvet curtain strung out on a railing by brass rings, we felt our heartstrings touched by the singing of "Shall We Gather at the River," "When the Roll Is Called Up Yonder," "There's a Land That Is Fairer Than Day," and, without giving too much thought to the picture it painted, "There Is a Fountain Filled with Blood." Sermons reminded us constantly of the uncertain length of our individual lives, and the inevitable arrival of the great day of judgment. When that day came, no church bells or fire whistle would allow a four-minute span of grace in which to repent, fling a few things into a suitcase, and get out of town. And there would be nowhere to go. Sinners would be caught red-handed, and too bad for them.

Oxford was Methodist, Methodist all the way. A college freshman once wrote home after his first week, "They are all Methodists here; it is a perfect hole of them! Outside of that, I like the place very much." They were not half so much followers of Christ as of John Wesley. The town had been named for the English university where he had received his education. He was their saint, and I think he would have approved of the systematic way in which they went about their religious observances.

Sunday school was not only for children; there were adult classes, too, and homework to do on the weekly lesson. Regular church attendance for everyone was taken as a matter of course. The main preaching service took place on Sunday morning, and after supper every family in town streamed back down for another sermon, even though in winter this meant navigating the dark streets by lantern-light. On Wednesday night, they did it again for a prayer meeting—same place, same crowd. The church's doors were open almost as often as they were closed, and all felt that they were leading godly lives in the completely Methodist fold of Oxford sheep. To my knowledge, I had never laid eyes on a Catholic. There was one Jew in town, professor of Old Testament and Hebrew at the college, but he was a converted Jew, married to a Gentile wife, and his family regularly filled a pew in our church.

I was eight years old before I even knowingly saw a Baptist, and it was the shock of my life. A recent graduate of the college, who

The New Church

ran the Arcade, had gone back to his hometown to be married, and the word went around that his bride, coming here to live, was a Baptist. I couldn't wait to see her. The very day that they arrived back in Oxford and settled into a cottage near the bookstore, I walked down there and sat under a tree in the street in front of the house to watch. I had a wait of several hours, for she was busy inside, but eventually she not only came out of the door, but into the yard, and walked about examining the shrubs and flower beds. I got a good look at her, front, back, and sides, and to my intense surprise, if I hadn't been told beforehand I should never have known that she wasn't a Methodist. When she went back into the house, I walked slowly home. I had something really to think about.

My conversion from a life of sin came soon after this. The regular routine of church services went on all year, but every spring, when the sap began to rise, religious emotionalism shifted into high gear, and there was a protracted meeting, or revival, with preaching each night for a week. Everybody came. All the adults in town were there, because they were the ones putting it on; all the children, because there was nobody left at home for them to stay with; all the college students, because if the truth were known, that week it was "the only game in town." They were doubly welcome, since they were "just entering manhood with its myriad temptations."

Some minister from out of town, renowned as a powerful orator and exhorter, would be brought in to spend the week with us, truly earning his stipend by delivering vigorous nightly sermons, and in the daytime consuming unbelievable amounts of chicken and layer cake in the homes of various church members.

The nightly services followed the same pattern. First, the place rocked with several revival songs to get everyone properly stirred up: "We're Marching to Zion," "O Happy Day That Fixed My Choice," "Revive Us Again," etc. Then came the sermon. After a full hour of impassioned pleading with us to forsake our sinful ways, the minister would retire to one of the high-backed pulpit chairs to rest and mop his forehead, for it was hot work wrestling with all those souls, while the congregation, led by the choir, indulged in another revival song.

There was nothing laughable here. It was a sincere appeal to one's deepest and most serious feelings; a person must have a heart of stone not to be stirred. Rested and rising, the minister then announced that he was going to "open the doors of the church" with an altar-call. Methodists have always felt that they were nearer to God when kneeling at His altar. So we all sang some hymn softly, such as "Almost Persuaded,"

Almost cannot avail
Almost is but to fail,
Sad, sad that bitter wail,
Almost, but lost!

while the converts of the evening edged over the knees of the other people in their pew and trooped down the aisle. It was a moving spectacle, and nothing to scoff at.

Night after spring night this went on. Sometimes it would take several services to touch a hard heart, but by the end of the revival week, just about everyone in town, students included, had usually succumbed and made the trip down the aisle to give the preacher his hand, either making a first commitment to God's service and hoping to have sins forgiven, or else renewing vows previously made to try to live a better life in the future. Maybe they kept to it, maybe they didn't, but at the time these meetings were certainly a rekindling of the spark within us, and everyone looked forward to the spring revival. As for the Emory students, at least it helped enliven that long dull stretch between Christmas vacation and commencement.

The spring that I was nine, an especially smashing revival took place, and there was a visiting minister with such a raucous voice that he wouldn't let me doze off as I usually did, my head in Mother's lap, so I found myself listening, and fascinated.

In his youth this man had been, he confessed to us, the worst of sinners; search the alleys, the byways, you could not find a worse. He had delighted in crimes so heinous he wouldn't even name them. He had us quivering with horror (and wishing he would go into more detail). And then one day, at a meeting just such as this one—into which he thought at the time he had wandered by chance (and to get out of the rain), but now knew that he had been divinely led—he was converted, and had cast it all behind him. He was born again! He looked with loathing at his former life, and decided then and there to enter the ministry and bring this great happiness to others.

I was absolutely entranced with his confession. So far as I knew I had never before looked at a sinner, but here was someone who had gone through the blackest mire, right to the bottom, and then up to the top again—for preachers were, of course, the best men in the world.

I was heartily in favor of the way he had worked it all out: to have a wild, delightful fling at every possible wicked thing that people always wanted to do but didn't dare to, and then to repent and not have to suffer any of the consequences. It was just the way I had thought I should like to live, except that there was always the horrible chance that I might die suddenly, as in an accident, or "before I wake," while still in my sinning stage. There had to be repentance if I expected to go to heaven, and not to go *there* would be terrible, for the rest of the family were all going, and it was as real a place to me as Covington.

Occasionally in the past I had worried a little for fear I might not make it. Living a completely blameless life wasn't easy. My sins were not what the song called "as scarlet"—I hadn't killed anybody, or stolen anything, or ever told an out-and-out lie. But fibs, yes—and I had certainly cut a few corners here and there.

Now, with the meeting going on every night and the whole town quivering with religious emotion, my conscience began pricking me into doing a little moral squirming. My past wasn't completely snow-white, and as to my future . . . well, I hadn't talked about it to anyone, so I was the only person who knew the things I was rather hoping to do in the future, sinful things that would be fun—always, of course, with repentance to save me before it was too late.

Then, one night after a stirring evangelistic sermon and the wailing singing of "Oh sinner, harden not your heart, be saved, oh, tonight!" the preacher stretched out his arms and said, "Will *you* be among the lost? Will *you* be someone who waited too long to repent?"—and he was looking right at me.

"Have you wanted to do wicked things?" he cried. "To have wanted in your heart to do them is as bad as actually having done them."

Somehow that man must have found out the plan I had half formulated for being wicked first, and then being saved. His eyes were boring right into me, telling me that it wouldn't work.

Then he "opened the doors of the church," as he always did at this point in the service, and urged all who desired not to be lost and damned forever to come down the aisle and give him their hand.

What else could I do? I scrambled across my mother at a clip too fast for her restraining grasp, and joined the procession down the aisle of repentant sinners, and with tears of remorse streaming down my face for my black past and those even blacker plans of my future life, gave the minister a loathsomely damp little hand. (Handkerchiefless, I had attempted to wipe both tears and nose on my trip down the aisle.)

Along with some full-grown fish, he had also caught a nine-year-old minnow in his net.

12

Sugar and Spice, Snaps and Snails

I used to hear grown people tell of comical experiences they had had, and I would wonder sadly what in the world I should do for something to talk about when I became grown, for nothing funny ever happened to me. How could I know, that grown up at last, it would be the "nothing" that I would tell about?

Children everywhere make collections of things, and our specialties were the smelly little colored tin tags that came on chewing tobacco plugs. Many men chewed tobacco, and the first thing they did after buying a new plug was to prize off the tag and let it fall in the dirt of the sidewalk. We also collected bird cards. Hot biscuits, requiring baking soda, were served at each meal in every home, and in every box of Arm & Hammer baking soda was a small colored picture of a bird. We brought our collections to school and swapped duplicates at recess.

But the main, and only remunerative, thing to collect was Octagon soap wrappers. The yellow cake of kitchen soap came in a heavy paper bearing the name "Octagon" in large letters. This word was to be cut out and saved as a coupon, for which the makers offered all sorts of premiums. One home did not use soap fast enough; it was necessary also to secure coupons from any neighbor who had no collecting child. The whole town was thoroughly canvassed, and we all had our "clients," on whom we called regularly for wrappers.

We pored over the coupon redemption book. There were all sorts of magnificent things, even bicycles (which we called "wheels"), but they required thousands of coupons and were too far out of the question even to dream of. But many a Christmas present came from the Octagon catalogue, and many a pocket-knife and string of glass beads. The thing for which I saved for months and months was a pair of buttonhole scissors, which took thirty-five coupons. No prouder child lived on earth than I when my mother opened the package on Christmas morning and told me it was the one thing in all the world that she needed and would rather have. She told the truth about needing them, for innumerable buttonholes did her patient fingers measure, snip open, and stitch around.

The "Stewart girls," Miss Emmie and Miss Sallie, used a lot of soap in the kitchen of their boardinghouse, and it was my chief port of call for wrappers. Because I was my mother's child and felt I could not take something and give no return, at the proper season I used to pick their violets for them. Neither Miss Sallie nor Miss Emmie was built for violet-picking, but Miss Emmie liked to keep great glass bowls of them on all the hall and parlor tables, so I picked them with long stems, and from time to time included a few leaves for accent. I would hitch my way along all the wide violet borders of all the Stewart walks, tying up the bunches with black sewing thread when they got too big to hold.

Besides the soap wrappers, Miss Emmie also gave me every month the Letty Lane paper dolls that came in the *Ladies' Home Journal*. At our house, we took only two magazines—both a dull black and white, and with no paper dolls. One was *Youth's Companion*, full of boys' stories of rescues and adventures and great deeds to inspire my brothers, for although they were fatherless and raised in a feminine household, Mother hoped they would grow up to be great and good *masculine* men. The other—and only Mother ever turned its pages—was the *Christian Advocate*, which retailed the goings-on of the Methodist Church, South, and its unattractive covers carried pictures of stern, unloved maiden missionaries who had journeyed to places on the other side of the world. Mother believed that it was every church member's duty to subscribe to the church paper, and she would have kept up that subscription if we were starving.

But the wonderful *L.H.J.* came to the Stewart sisters every month, and having no little girl of their own, they always tore its sheet of colored paper dolls out and gave it to me. I didn't see how they could bear to part with it, and each month, on the walk down to get it, my heart thumped with terror that they had come to their senses and decided to keep it.

First there appeared Letty Lane herself, a little girl just about my age, with long golden curls and at least eight dresses; then Letty's cousin, equally beautiful and equally endowed with clothes; her best friend; her mother; her aunt; her grown sister; and on and on, as the months marched. They were all in the loveliest colors. The little girls had party dresses and pale blue and pink hair ribbons and sashes, while the ladies had ruffles and strips of embroidery down their skirts. I would have picked violets until my fingers were bones for the magnificent gift of these paper doll sheets!

The reason that they were so precious was that most of our paper dolls were not the sort whose dresses could be taken off and on, and were not colored; only Letty Lane's were like this. Paper dolls were all the rage with little girls. We cut out our usual families of "papes" from mail-order catalogues, classified them by age and sex, and kept the different members of the family in separate pages of old magazines.

My family was named McKnight, the most elegant name I could think up. All the ladies were Mrs. McKnight, all the men

The Stewart House

her husband; there were several boys and girls of different ages, and two babies—one in long clothes, one in short. I found two pictures of a man wearing glasses; he became the doctor, with only those two suits, poor soul, for I never found any more bespectacled men. But the McKnights were a healthy crew and the doctor wasn't called in very often, so he didn't wear his clothes out as fast as Mr. McKnight did. Eventually Mr. McKnight became rather limp in the middle from being constantly bent so he could sit in the vine on the front porch, which was his office where he went every day to make money.

He was very rich. I gave him a salary of $100 a month, until my friends Mary and Frances rose up and protested that nobody ever made that much money and if I wasn't going to play sensibly, they wouldn't play at all. So Mr. McKnight's salary was reduced to $20, which still seemed quite a lot (none of the three of us had the faintest idea about money), but at any rate, the figure got by them.

The mail-order catalogues that we cut dolls from had an annoying custom of picturing people in groups. We had a rule that the person must be whole or we wouldn't cut it out, and often the nicest dress on the whole page was half hidden by several other people in a group. This was a heartbreak when a beautiful, desirable lady had somebody else standing near her and hiding part of her skirt, or one of her arms. Once a particularly lovely one that I could not bring myself to give up seemed to be without an arm from the elbow down, so I had a happy thought. I cut her out anyway and created a new member of the family: Mrs. McKnight's sister, who had her arm taken off in an accident on the railroad. From that time on, I even searched for one-armed ladies, with the right or left indiscriminately missing, until one day Mary discovered this, and after that I was kept strictly to the same arm. My suggested solution of *two* sisters in the same accident, one of whom had her left arm cut off and the other the right, was indignantly rejected.

We spent a great deal of time behind the scenes as impresarios, cutting out new ones, gluttonously recounting them after each session of cutting out, and swapping with each other. Postal cards cost a penny in those days, and an excellent investment was to send one to Bellas Hess or the National Cloak and Suit Company. "Dear sirs: Please send me your spring and summer catalogue." Far away in Chicago, they had no way of knowing that I was only a little girl with itchy scissors waiting to whack their catalogues to pieces, and not a grown lady in need of suits and dresses. For a long time I signed the cards honestly "Very truly yours, Miss Florence Stone," and then I suddenly thought they would be less apt to suspect me if I were married and looking for clothes for an entire family, so I changed the unformed nine-year-old "Miss" to an equally wobbly "Mrs." Although I sent them no order for clothes, the catalogues continued to come, spring and summer, fall and winter, and I continued to snip and count and swap. I was always fearful, however, that those great stores might have detectives who would figure out that I was no Mrs. and would send to punish me, and after mailing a request I never felt quite safe until the catalogue arrived unaccompanied by the constable's knock.

If I couldn't go off to another girl's house to play and no one came to mine, and if I was desperate for company, I could as a last resort always walk to the edge of our lot and call to see if the little boy next door would come over. He was two years younger, and each of us would have preferred someone of our own age and sex, but he had some good points. He lived nearer than anybody else, and there was no rigmarole about asking permission, for we were generally in sight in the yard, and if either of our mothers wanted us, they called from the porch or out of the window. Also, since I was older and bigger than he was, if I grew weary of his company, to make him go home was a simple matter.

He and I would cut branches from the tall chinaberry tree that grew on the line between our houses, to bend and make Indian bows with a piece of string; the foot-long straight leaf spines made excellent arrows with which we tried to wing each other. He had a pocketknife that one of his older brothers had discarded, not as sharp as a Wilkinson sword certainly, but still a knife. We went through endless games of mumblety-peg in the grass with it, blunting it still more each time it was flipped into the ground. We whittled pens from pithy sticks, made purple ink from ripe pokeberries, and wrote mysterious unsigned notes to our mothers, to be left around the house, warning of coming disasters.

We tunneled through the dirt under the plank siding in our coal cellar and wriggled grimily toward what was our robbers' cave. There were no jewels or gold or quartered corpses in view once we got inside, only lumps of coal; the difficult and mysterious way of getting in without coming through the door was really all there was to it.

With no snow, we could never pelt each other with snowballs, but in the spring, when new clover grew lush under the peach trees in Mother's little orchard, we used to snatch off handfuls of it until we each had an immense green pile, and then engage in clover fights until our supply was exhausted.

When there was no one at all to play with, not even boys, there were plenty of things to do alone. There were always dolls, and paper dolls, and there were my three fairy books, which I read to shreds and which put romantic ideas into my head about being really a princess of royal blood, and apt at any time to be called upon to exchange the Griffin house for a castle. It had happened to Cedric Errol! But even if I couldn't be a princess, it was consoling to know that, after all, none of the other Oxford girls were either. Many times I weighed the differences between being a grown-up or a child, and always decided that I was glad that I was the latter, for although grown people had the advantage of making all the rules, and seemed to keep themselves occupied, it was with what looked to me like rather dull things, while for us there were millions of exciting activities always waiting to be plunged into, and the days were not long enough. Each night I put myself to sleep planning what I should do tomorrow.

Children in Oxford were necessary, respected citizens, playing an important part in the town's life. A network of them crisscrossed town every day as messengers, bearing notes and waiting to take the answers back. Other than placing them practically in charge of Oxford's communications system, the grown-ups had laid down two main occupations for children: getting an education, and growing up to be fine men and women. The first filled the mornings, and we clop-clopped obediently down the path beaten hard by the feet of Oxford children before us. But when school was out, we and our peers were in charge of working out the other, and we threw ourselves into the delightful business of being "a dear little girl" or "a regular boy." And when something happened to turn out disastrously, we were never dubbed delinquents, or marched off to a psychiatrist or a counselor, but simply given a good whipping. Corporal punishment for a child was not looked on as brutality, but as the occasional necessary duty of parents. No one grew up without a few whippings. Sometimes one was even administered to a boy at school for a deed considered especially heinous, such as turning over a bottle of ink on a little girl's dress. Even then it was not done in school time, however, with everybody "assembled to witness punishment," but after school was out and in the privacy of the principal's office, and everyone was very, very sorry.

My brother Harry was once supposed to be thus whipped—I don't remember for what, but I know that I went home that day in tears, with all my little girl friends trotting along beside me in sympathy. We needn't have worried. Before any corporal punishment, there was always a sorrowful lecture, with admonitions to lead a better life in the future, and Harry was such an engaging little rascal that before the sermon was over he had talked the principal out of further punishment, and came jauntily home, whistling. A boy not as glib as Harry, who had to go through with it all, usually placed a book down the back of his trousers beforehand, and began screaming loudly before the first lick fell, so that even a whipping at school never amounted to much. There was talk of trips made by bad boys to the woodshed with their fathers for a taste of his belt, but with no father at our house we never experienced this. And I read once about a mother's taking a hairbrush to her daughter. This puzzled me; switches were the only thing used for punishment at our house. Why would brushing your hair be a punishment?

Whenever Mother considered that we had done something really bad, such as direct disobedience that had brought bad consequences, she followed the advice of the Good Book in not sparing the rod; we were not to grow up "spoiled." Her trembling little talks to us beforehand about trying to do right always and grow up to be good people were worse than any switching. "Switch me, Mother, but *please* don't *talk* to me!" I once begged her. She used limber little switches from a wretched peach tree in the back yard that never had any peaches on it, and she had a perfectly horrid habit of sending us out to cut our own. This gave the culprit the decision as to its size. Should we penitently bring in a stout one that would last a while, or be a coward and choose a very slender one that one or two whacks would wear out? Yet even those would sting through our heavy cotton stockings.

Small boys and girls seldom mixed if they could help it, being rather contemptuous of each other's undertakings and games. Whenever we girls tried to kiss an elbow in order to turn into the other sex, we were thankful that it didn't work, while the boys didn't even try.

Girls were constantly urged to be "ladylike," and to this end, they all "took." "Who do you take from?" was the ungrammatical way of asking who your music teacher was. My mother was probably the only lady in town who hadn't "taken" as a girl, but she had been the middle daughter of a minister's family and got the little end of the stick. She had a true if untrained voice, so our house often rang with her songs as she went about the housework or pedaled away on her sewing machine. They usually had romantic, sad themes: beautiful Mabel Claire would no more gather roses to twine in her dark brown hair, the young gazelle was sure to die, the maiden in the Blue Alsatian Mountains withered like a flower that was waiting for the rain. Mother regretted her lack of musical training, and gladly accepted the offer of an aunt to give me lessons and let me practice on her piano half an hour a day. I was wild with joy, for I thought I should be able to walk out after the first lesson and be able to play. It was the bitterest disappointment of my life to find out that that wasn't the way it was done. Aunt Sallie's piano and I hated each other. It seemed to be gritting its ivory teeth at me, and I gritted mine right back.

No boy ever "took"; it would have been regarded as sissy. The nearest he ever came to making music was to whistle, and the only two musical instruments he tolerated were two he could carry in his pocket—a Jew's harp, and a Sears Roebuck fifteen-cent harmonica.

Acquiring muscle in their upper arms was the thing boys in Oxford were interested in, constantly pushing up their sleeves and checking to see how it was getting on, boastfully inviting both male competitors and admiring little girls to "feel my muscle." They tested their strength by coming up behind little girls and lifting them off the ground, and before they could actually do it, small boys kept trying to lift their laughing mothers.

Because the boys liked to have privacy for their times together, when they plotted things, they would build themselves a house in a tree, or a hut behind some shrubs, with a notice, "Keep out this means U". They went off together in gangs to the swimming hole in Dried Indian Creek, for a ramble in the country to set rabbit traps and find birds' eggs, or, if there were enough of them, to the Palmer playground for baseball.

Girls, not being handy with hammer and nails, never built anything. We didn't like to be shut up in a hut, and preferred playing with our dolls on the end of a porch, where we could see what was going on. We doted on playing personal "talk games," like last-go-trade, and truth-upon-honor, both of which usually ended in hurt feelings or downright animosity, with paper dolls gathered up and visitors sailing off home in a huff.

There were never hurt feelings between boys. They preferred for a game or project to continue, but if a row did arise, after a few glares and dares of "smell my fist" and "kiss my foot," the belligerents would go for each other, ending with a bloody nose or a black eye until one of them was ready to "holler calf rope." There were no hard feelings.

But most children's get-togethers came to an amicable end when evening began to close in. Children weren't out after dark, for in unlighted Oxford it was dark indeed, and there was no place like home.

There was one day a year when boys were expected and allowed to indulge in devilment—Halloween, of course. It was not a trick-or-treat night, with the very little children in costume going from door to door, for there were no treats, only rather horrid tricks played on householders by the biggest boys, which were often plain vandalism. After dark they gathered and roamed the town, lifting gates off their hinges, putting tick-tacks on windows, doing damage to anything left in the yards, and (their prime offense, and the one in which they delighted the most) overturning outhouses. Sometimes they even carried them around and left them in the front yards.

One year the older Palmer boys invaded the fowl-yard of the house next door to the school and plucked all the feathers off the two turkeys there. The next morning, when the owner saw the two birds walking around bare, she was horrified—as well she might be, for turkeys, appearances to the contrary, are very delicate birds and easily catch a fatal cold. But these were saved. Their owner went right to work and made little gray flannel coverall suits, and until Thanksgiving, when a worse fate than walking around bare awaited them, they paraded the back yard dressed in their new outfits, to the delight of the Palmer children who passed on the way to school.

The benighted heathen in eastern lands for whom we in the children's missionary society felt such concern, and who in their turn felt concern for the spark of life in any sort of a creature, even a flea, would have been horrified at the things we "whose souls were lighted with wisdom from on high" carelessly and thoughtlessly did to living wild things. We would tie a string to a harmless June bug's leg and fly him like a kite until he died from exhaustion or pulled a leg off; we imprisoned the twilight's glowing lightning bugs in a jar where they blinked out their lives during the night. Boys robbed birds' nests, taking every single egg. They would pierce each end with a pin, and when they blew into one end, all the insides came out the other. They then made a collection of the empty eggs, admiring the blue or speckled shells, and never giving a thought to the little robins or brown thrashers that would not have a chance to fly and sing. By making a fine collection, they felt they were nature lovers, and did not realize that they were murderers. There were no wildlife societies to tell us how dreadful this was. Milliners and their lady customers showed as little concern for bird life as the children did. "Cruelty to animals" meant to us only whipping mules and horses and tying tin cans to stray dogs' tails—and we wouldn't have been mean enough to do such things for anything.

As for birds, they took care of themselves. There were plenty of wild berries and seeds and worms for them to eat, so people didn't have to do anything about feeding them. We led our lives; the birds led theirs.

Dogs and cats were another matter. Every boy had to have a

dog as a companion; every house a cat to keep the mice down. A cat was a part of the household equipment, like flypaper. These animals were never bought at a pet shop, never pedigreed, but were to be had for the asking from a neighbor's house. Since there was no tampering with the adult animals, new ones were constantly being born. If the supply got too numerous, the hired man took a sack of newborns down to the creek while the children were in school.

The care of pets was not onerous. They ate bones and the leftovers scraped from dinner plates, and cats supplemented this with baby rabbits or, if the house was near either of the two little streams that flowed at the sides of the village, with minnows. No dog had to be walked; dogs got all the exercise they needed without being led along like a slave on a chain. There was not a leash in town. To lead a dog's life meant in Oxford to lead a contented one. To be a dog was to enjoy a status that afforded unmitigated freedom and pleasure.

13

Black Folks

There were almost as many black people in Oxford as there were whites; they furnished plenty of cooks, butlers, nursemaids, stable- and yardmen, and washwomen. Everyone who needed help or a job could find it. Neither the white master nor the mistress of a house ever held a hoe or a rake in their hands, and had not even a nodding acquaintance with weeds or fallen leaves, for all yard work was done by a black man or boy. If the family didn't have a full-time man, there were any number of young or old who would come for one or more regular days a week, or for a specific job such as planting the garden.

They were usually called "colored folks." No one said "blacks" or pronounced the name of the race as "Neegroes." "Darky" was often heard, but it was not said in derision; the term had an informal, almost affectionate, tone—something like referring to children as "kids." "Nigger" was used by them much more than it was by whites. They might say to one of their own race, "You black nigger, you!"—meaning someone utterly worthless and good for nothing. Some of the men were lazy and quite content to be supported by a wife's hard work as cook or washwoman, but none of them was corrupt. Occasionally the town record books posted a fine for fighting between two of them, but it was always a personal argument, and women and girls were always perfectly safe anywhere at any time. There were never assaults or burglaries.

Black and white families had been bound together for generations, since before the Civil War, something like the old clan and
sept system in the highlands of Scotland. The Gaithers, for instance, had always worked for the Stewarts, the Curingtons for
the Branhams, the Wrights for the Stones. They were "their families." There was friendship and loyalty to each other. Black children were often named after members of their white families. My
father, who, having practiced law for a while, was called "Colonel," a courtesy-title for all lawyers in the South, was asked to be
godfather for one such baby. When he stood at the altar in the
black church, he was astounded to hear the child's baptismal name
given as "Colonel-Will." "Cunnel-will" he was called all his life.

Servants never "lived in." They carried on their own private lives
in a settlement called Shakerag, on the edge of the town proper,
where there were forty-six property-holders. (There were seventy-
two white homeowners in Oxford.) Shakerag was made up of a
small number of nice-looking little houses, and a larger number
of rather pathetic, weathered cabins. "Uncle" Frank Brown's was
a typical one, valued at $60, and taxed twenty-seven cents an-
nually. (By comparison, the white-pillared Branham house, one of
the finest in Oxford, was valued at $2,065 and taxed at $9.30.)

In the otherwise bone-bare Shakerag yards, there was usually a
flower bed or two, outlined with whitewashed rocks, and the
shelves along the porch rails had tin cans full of bright petunias or
geraniums. There would be a ramshackle privy leaning at an angle
at a too-short distance from the house, and a carelessly kept vegetable garden—more or less fenced to keep out chickens and
hogs—a few peach trees, perhaps a fig tree, and always a chinaberry or two shading the yard.

The settlement was named for its billowing clotheslines; "taking
in" the white folks' clothes for washing was the chief occupation
of women who were not employed in homes as cooks and nurses.

It provided the means for any able-bodied black woman, however unskilled and ignorant, to make a living (and often support a husband and several children). During the early part of the week you might have thought that an army with banners was encamped in Shakerag; it was a gay sight.

A student's laundry went out with that of the family where he lived. Meals, room, and washing were included in the very small sum paid each week to his landlady. No white family ever did its own washing; nor was it done on the place. Even at the time when we were poorest, the soiled clothes were regularly "counted out" each week, and then carried off to Shakerag. The women who came to get the clothes stalked off with the long splint baskets balanced on their heads, one hand on a hip, and one on a side of the basket to steady it. Men never carried things on their heads; if they collected the wash, they drove in a wagon or trundled a wheelbarrow.

Mother had written her name with indelible ink in the hems of plain look-alike white sheets and pillowcases, but although a washwoman might work for several families, she knew to whom each garment that passed through her hands belonged, and never delivered any to the wrong house. The wash went out on Monday, and was supposed to come back on Saturday, but occasionally a few items were not delivered until the following Monday at pick-up time. If my best white dress, for instance, failed to appear on Saturday, there was sure to be a special children's service at the black church on Sunday, and my dress would be needed by the washwoman's daughter, who was my age. "A rainy week when things jes' wouldn't dry" would be given as the cause of the delay. There was not a thing we could do about it. Miss Emmie Stewart's shirtwaists and skirts often had a similar religious experience, and her Cleo said happily in explanation, "You see, me and Miss Emmie is hipted and busted jes' the same."

Out in the washwoman's yard, under the chinaberry tree, stood a bench on which were set the round galvanized washtubs, with the scrubbing boards standing up in them. Nearby, blue smoke rose from a fire with a black iron pot perched lopsided over it, and here the clothes were boiled until the colors were considered to be sufficiently wrecked. (Before any new colored garment left home, however, any housewife who knew what was what had already "set the colors" as much as possible, by soaking it in strong cold salt water overnight.)

Wringing was done either by hand-twisting or with a wringer that you fed material into while turning a crank to press out the water. Regardless of the method used, soaking-wet double bed sheets were heavy. There were clotheslines strung haphazardly from tree to tree, but, alas, the most readily available drying facilities were the rusty strands of barbed-wire fence stretched along the patch where the collards and turnip greens grew. Every washwoman alive would stoutly deny that she hung clothes on barbed wire, but it was the only place where they could acquire the little three-cornered snags that decorated every piece that passed through the washwoman's hands. It was so convenient: it was *there*. Everything had to be ironed. The heavy irons were heated on top of the kitchen stove, with one put back to heat while the other was being used.

Besides the cook and the washwoman, and of course a nurse if there was a baby or small children, some households, especially if possessed of a horse or cow, employed a full-time man who saw to the animals, did the garden, washed the windows, waxed floors, and beat the rugs. These last were taken out and hung over a line in the back yard and beaten with a flail, something like a stout flyswatter, made expressly for the purpose and capable of delivering a mighty whack. The dust would rise in clouds from rugs that had only been broom-swept.

At the Griffin place, "Uncle" Frank Brown came to us one day a week for the garden, and to do odd jobs, for seventy-five cents a day. When the garden or fruit trees were bearing, he supplemented this bountifully, and even during the winter, besides a hearty meal in the kitchen, he always had something to "tote" home. "Totin'" was a well-established custom, and should be remembered if the wages paid seem horrifyingly small. The entire family of the cook was usually fed from her employer's kitchen; her husband or one of the older family members appeared about dusk and sat in the kitchen waiting to walk home with her, always having his own supper there first, and helping her carry off enough provender to feed the rest at home.

Since ice chests barely contained enough room for milk and meat, unless the amount left over was enough to be used at another meal the next day, it was just as well for it to be eaten by someone right then. But because cooks did not always recognize clearly the difference between cooked food for which there was no refrigeration and staples on the pantry shelves, locks were necessary on pantry doors. Occasionally the mistress would investigate an especially large sack as it started out her back door, and remove perhaps half a dozen sweet potatoes or such, but even when this happened there were no hard feelings on either side. The objective was for every meal to be completely eaten up, with no leftovers to spoil. Between the white family in the dining room, the kitchen help and their families, and the animals that were given the scraps on plates, this was usually done.

When an Oxford family moved away, the cook or the children's nurse would often go along. This afforded servants a trip into the outside world, and was also the means of getting jobs for a stream of relations in the new town, too.

The black folks had their own cemetery, school, and church. They infinitely preferred running their own affairs, especially in the church, where they shouted, spoke out "in tongues," and praised the Lord volubly when they "felt the spirit." The restrained worship at the white church was not for them. Rather than sermons from great preachers, they wanted fellowship and the freedom to express themselves when they "got religion." Since they were always busy getting their employers' noon dinners on Sundays, their main service was in the evening, when the congregational singing was really something to hear.

Sometimes an invitation was extended to white friends to attend the black church when there was to be a song service. Those always turned out to be expensive as well as embarrassing entertainments, for the whites were always welcomed by name, and were immediately waited on punctiliously by the deacons with the collection plates, while the congregation twisted around in their seats and every eye was fixed upon their guests. After the deacons had marched up the aisle with the plates, the "take" was counted audibly, the total announced from the pulpit, and if not as much had been contributed as was required for some special project, the minister would give notice that the plate was coming around again, and he hoped that this time, the sum, named exactly, would be forthcoming. With your own cook sitting there with her eyes on you, you could not let her down before her friends, and have that proud grin turn to humiliation because her white folks were so stingy. Inviting white people to attend a song service was a cagey way to raise money for any project. But the singing was worth it.

One of my most beloved friends when I was a little girl was an aged toothless black woman we called "Aunt" Ellen, one of the Gaither clan. She was quite an old woman, with scant gray hair braided into little two-inch plaits that were wrapped in string and led into each other, so that her entire head was one web of tiny plaits. She always wore a bandanna tied around it. Her little cabin was not in Shakerag but at the back of the parsonage lot, and faced our house across the street. The parson's youngest daughter, Mary, was my best friend, and we shared "Aunt" Ellen, vying with each other as to which of us could do the most for her. Whenever I had any special treat, part of it always was carried across the street to her cabin; I almost always trotted over to take her my dessert on Sunday—quite a sacrifice, too, for it was the only day of the week we had dessert, and I had a sweet tooth that was never fully satisfied. So little in this life came "Aunt" Ellen's way that she could not be blamed for being a greedy, fawning old soul, but Mary and I saw no flaw in her character, felt honored that she would accept our offerings, and were rapt listeners to her steady stream of talk.

We were entranced with her living arrangements. She cooked on the open hearth of the only room of her cabin, and we would squat down beside her on the floor in front of the fire, watching her pat and mold a hoecake into shape. She was not overly clean about her person, her dishes, or her food, but with regard to this last she comforted herself and us, when she shared one of her hoecakes right from the ashes, with the old saying that "you have to eat a peck of dirt in your life." Her walls were pasted over with old newspapers, a wall covering of which we heartily approved. We never tired of circling the room, reading the articles, and looking at the pictures. Sometimes they were pasted on sideways, and even upside down. She told us this was an old Gullah custom, to divert any witches who might enter between midnight and cockcrow.

"Aunt" Ellen was a washwoman by profession; her washtub sat outside on a bench under a sycamore tree, and it was when I was about ten that she taught me there how to wash stockings. This was no gentle swishing back and forth through a bowl of frothy suds; you really put your back into it. You were, of course, starting with a stout material that you could batter; present-day gossamer hose would not take the treatment we gave.

First you washed them on the right side, rubbing vigorously against a cake of yellow soap, then turned them wrong side out and did it again, just as thoroughly. Then you put them in clear rinsing water, rinsing first on one side, then turning them and rinsing thoroughly again, rubbing good and hard during both rinses. By this time, my fingertips were white and shriveled, but it wasn't over yet; now came inspection. If you saw a grain of sand, or a spot of lint, or a fleck of soap, in they went again. No wonder mothers were constantly sitting by a darning basket piled high with the family stockings; what havoc we didn't wreak on them in wear, the washings did.

Like many old women who have raised a "passel" of children without benefit of running constantly to a doctor for advice, "Aunt" Ellen had a number of her own simple prescriptions for minor ills. One was for hiccups: nine swallows of water. It works, too. Drinking that many swallows in rapid succession without a breath is not as easy as it sounds, and between counting to be sure you have done enough (and not a single one over), and making the necessary physical exertion for swallowing, by the time you have glugged down the last one, you find you are worn out, with no strength for hiccuping anymore. For a nosebleed, you must drop a key down your back, and lay a strip of paper between your lip and upper gum.

"Aunt" Ellen, like all those old-time black women, was very religious and "preachy." "The Bad Place" was as actual to her as Shakerag and "the Bad Man" a real character. She would lower her voice, and glance over her shoulder if she spoke of him. She told Mary and me with rolling eyeballs that the reason you never see blue jays on Friday is because they are agents of the Bad Man, and that is the day they go to report to him about any wicked things they have seen boys and girls do during the week. "Watch out for jay birds!"

"Never say 'hello'" was another of her admonitions. "Hell—that's the Bad Place. Instead, you must say 'hey-o.'" And say "hey-o" Mary and I did, scrupulously.

When the time came for us to move away from Oxford, "Aunt" Ellen was one of the people I hated most to part with, and almost the last thing I did that morning was to run across to her cabin and throw myself into her shriveled old arms for a sobbing good-bye hug.

14

Wherewithal We Were Clothed

The teen-aged girls who were out-of-town guests at Emory commencements brought along a variety of lacy dresses and hats, sometimes made entirely of lace or embroidery stretched over a wire frame, and pink and white ruffled parasols. These last were so numerous that for a long time I believed that the right to bear a parasol came automatically with being sixteen or so.

Oxford residents themselves had only the necessary things, and very little else. The ladies, almost all of them frugal faculty wives, did not go around swathed in lace, and twirling coquettish parasols. "Adequate" clothing was the objective, and when that level was reached, nothing more needed to be added. Nothing was ever replaced just because everybody in town had seen it. We recognized each other's garments as old friends, were glad to see them again at the beginning of a new season, and were interested in any added bits or rearrangements.

The one exception to "adequate and only the necessary" was the item called "a fur." But that wasn't really an extravagance, because it not only lasted a lifetime, but could also be willed to a relative. Several Oxford ladies had, in fact, inherited theirs.

A fur was a neckpiece made of a deceased animal—say, a fox, with his bushy tail still hanging on one end, and his head, with yellow-brown glass eyes, glaring at the other. A lady in one of these, calling on my mother, laid it on a chair. Fascinated, I investigated, and found that it fastened by having the animal's jaws, neatly lined with brown silk, snap over one of his dangling paws on the other end. A fur neckpiece was sometimes accompanied by a matching muff—another animal pelt, head and all, going into this. A muff might be roly-poly or flat, with the head and dangling paws decorating the front. But a fur and muff were luxurious extras, and not every woman had them. In Oxford's climate, fur wasn't really needed for warmth; wool was perfectly adequate.

The main thing we asked of clothes was to keep us warm in winter and cool in summer, so their texture changed with the seasons. On winter nights, with nobody awake to stoke the fires, the town curled up in flannel, sometimes even with footies, too. Men and boys slept in nightshirts to their ankles, for pajamas were still far away in their native homes of India and Persia. When they did reach America, they were only for men at first—women never wore pants.

On rising in those cold bedrooms, everybody leaped immediately into long johns. The great fall and spring decision in every family was when to begin wearing them and when to take them off. So important was this question that the handbook of a girls' college to which some Palmer graduates had gone, expressing the college's responsibility *in loco parentis*, warned, "The young lady pupils should *by no means* neglect to put on adequate winter underwear at the approach of cold weather."

The other attribute of clothes, along with helping to regulate temperature, was modesty—perhaps excess modesty, for in both summer and winter, just about all of a lady except her face and hands was hidden from view. Even her own husband wasn't allowed to see too much; her cool summer nightgowns were made of a white cotton material stout enough not to be transparent, to the ankle in length, with sleeves to the wrist, and a stand-up ruffle at the neck. Negligees were called "wrappers" or "Mother Hubbards"—this latter a long-sleeved, high-necked yoke from which shapeless yards of material fell to the heels.

Underclothes for everyone were white, as were also bed clothes and table linen. Underclothes came in units of a half-dozen at a minimum, to allow a garment to go out and come back from the weekly wash. Not even around home did a woman ever go without a corset. That indispensable resembled a medieval knight's armor, reaching up high and extending down low, and stiffly and unyieldingly whaleboned every inch of the way. It hooked up the front, but the wide-open back was laced across with a long corset-string, and so could be drawn in or let out to produce the requisite curves, and provide the overall effect of "pleasingly plump." No one dieted. It nipped a woman in at the waistline, and encouraged a swell above and below; bust and hips were the things to be stressed—the wisp of a waist in between was preferably negligible. Directly over this came the corset-cover, a dainty white lawn concoction, with its fullness drawn up with baby ribbon run in and out of eyelets, which created a bunchiness to help swell out that general above-the-waist bulge, but concealed all definite outline of breasts. A solid rampart was to be presented up there, not two pyramids.

Below the waist came what were frankly called "drawers," or there was a top-and-bottom combination named kittenishly a "teddy." Over the fundamentals were voluminous petticoats, perhaps two or three, but certainly enough so that dressed in a thin summer dress a lady couldn't be "seen through." Ruffles on the bottom were not only ironed, but, for the more stylish, fluted as well. This last was a provocative crimping made by a special iron owned by the washwomen of the best families. In winter, a petticoat of taffeta made a lovely rustling—"like autumn leaves across the grass." A one-piece combination of corset-cover and petticoat, made in long sections and sewed together with no waistline, was called a "princess slip."

Necks were never left completely bare. Elderly ladies pinned a black velvet band around their throats; shirtwaists and dresses always had a stand-up collar band several inches high. Shirtwaists and dresses never opened in the front, which meant that someone had to be available to "do them up the back." Somebody always was; ladies did not live alone. If there was no husband or other member of the family available, there would be a woman servant to insert the buttons in the buttonholes out of reach and sight in the small of the back. Buttons as well as hooks and eyes were the fasteners. Snaphooks were looked at askance when they first appeared. People felt it was taking a great risk to use them in vital closings, for even the most genteel lady could with one deep breath pop open a whole row of them.

Since everything opened up the back, there was left a broad expanse of bosom to be decorated in the front, and this was done with a lady's gold watch, fastened on one shoulder with a fleur-de-lys pin called a chatelaine.

Skirts, descending to the ground, were gored, snugly fitted at the firmly corseted waist, then flaring out below the hips. On the front panel was often a large geometric design in soutache braid; wide bands of embroidery or lace insertion were let in down the sides.

Dresses required many hours to make and many yards of material, six for a plain dress, eight for a ruffled one. Many of the more popular materials have since passed out of memory: foulard, Indian head, ratiné, pongee, batiste, mull, voile, nainsook, georgette crepe and crepe de chine, organdy, dimity, china silk. Tulle and malines were diaphanous materials often draped around one's best hats or around shoulders to fill in a low-necked formal evening gown.

At the apex of all this smotheration of clothing, each lady was topped with a great mass of hair, as long and thick as she could grow—or supplement, if the natural crop was scanty. All ladies had long hair, often to the waist. (The French writer Colette could twist her toes in hers!) Hair brushes were plied religiously; fifty strokes, or even a hundred, were required before a female could go to bed with a clear conscience. Hair was "done up" on top of the head with a multitude of hairpins or combs. There was a roach comb for pompadours, little side combs fluffed out hair around the face, a back comb took care of the errant wisps that so often escaped from the topknot. To wave the hair around the face, many ladies spent all the nights of their lives lying uncomfortably on a dozen or so little hard knobs of kid or metal curlers. There was also a curling iron that was held over a lamp flame until it zipped to a wet finger.

If a woman's hair was not very thick, she helped it out with a switch, or a circular wire "rat," which resembled a transparent sausage. To wear this, she placed it on her head like a crown, then gathered all the hair up over it into a topknot. It gave a rather severe effect, but was neat. Often combings were saved in a "hair receiver"—a round jar with a hole in the lid—to make a switch, which not only meant that it would be a perfect match, but was regarded as being more delicate than wearing the hair of an unknown.

The only thing a lady needed to take care of her own hair was a cake of soap and soft rainwater, if she had caught some; otherwise, a pinch of baking soda in well water would be almost as good. Packer's tar soap was the favorite, with a squirt of lemon juice in the rinse water to get all the suds out. Hair dye? Never! Actresses and "bad women" in red-light districts might stoop to this, but no dyed strand of hair ever crowned the head of an honest woman.

In summer, Old Sol himself was the hair dryer, as a woman sat in the yard with a towel around her shoulders. In the winter, she sat on the floor in front of the grate fire, and for a day or so afterward would truthfully say, "I've just washed my hair and I can't do a thing with it."

Because of all those buns of hair, whether false or bona fide, a hat could not hug the head itself, but had to perch on top, so hatpins were necessary. On each bureau sat a hatpin holder—a little china column with holes in the top to stick them in, like an elongated salt shaker. A hatpin would be eight to twelve inches long, with a really sharp point at one end (for it must go through the hat itself, sometimes twice), and at the other end an ornamental knob.

Retrimming one's hat, or even doing it over from the beginning, was a regular occurrence. Shapes for home trimming, and all the necessary decorations, were for sale, and by the time a lavish and imaginative hand got through decorating a hat, it was a fearful and wonderful concoction! The brims were loaded down like a tea tray with flowers or small fruits (cherries were favorites) or ribbons, and even the kindest, most humane ladies would walk out contentedly in a hat decorated with birds' feathers—both wings clipped on the sides like Mercury's, and sometimes the entire little corpse of a red-wing blackbird, oriole, or dove nestled down among loops of ribbon. Face veils, with spots, were often drawn tightly over the face from a hat brim.

No one really needed more than two hats—one for winter and one for summer. The trimming might be rearranged over and over, added to or subtracted from, as it became limp, but as long as the basic hat held out, it was considered adequate unless some catastrophe occurred, such as the cat's having kittens in it. This happened to my mother once. We were indebted to that multiple birth for bringing Mother out of mourning.

When a close relative died, ladies always "went into mourning." There was an understood period for "full mourning," which meant wearing only black, with handkerchiefs, visiting cards, and stationery all black-bordered. (Queen Victoria's black borders for her mother's death were increased to almost an inch after Prince Albert died.) Men wore a black band sewn on a sleeve of every coat. Even the children "showed respect"; to my grandmother Stone's funeral in the Old Church, my cousin Emma Louise and I, who were very small girls, wore white dresses and black taffeta hair ribbons. After "full mourning" came "half mourning," when a woman might wear white, or lavender, and then gradually make her way back into colors. But Mother's heart was in full mourning, and would be all the rest of her life; she had no desire to check on the required number of months, or to change when the time came. She stayed in full mourning for about five years. My earliest memory of her is a slight little figure in black.

The same hat sufficed Mother for both summer and winter. It was what was called a toque—brimless, close fitting—with a deep mourning veil pinned around it with black-headed pins, and hanging down the back. There is no telling how long she might have made it do, if our cat, in her search for a suitable place for her accouchement, had not selected the box in which it was kept, and nudged off the lid.

Men's clothes at this time were deadly dull to look at, with no bright colors, no dashing plaids. There were no variations with blazers or sport coats. Suits came in three-piece sets, with a vest of the same material with each suit. Sometimes two pairs of pants were included. The Sunday best was always of dark blue serge, and it got very shiny with wear.

Because of their overload of starch, high, uncomfortable collars were kept separate from shirts, and lay coiled like snakes in a round leather collar box on each gentleman's chiffonier. Every morning, after a man had survived the danger of cutting his throat by shaving with a straight-edge razor, he went into the gyrations of prying open board-like buttonholes and inserting half of a collar button. Once the shirt and collar had been firmly married to each other, and he had confided his poor neck to their relentless prison, he fitted his big hunting-case watch to its little watch pocket in the band of his trousers, or in his vest, and crowned his appearance by inserting a stickpin in his four-in-hand necktie. With this stickpin's selection, even the mousiest and most modest of men cut quite a dash, for its head could be a representation of anything under the sun: a horseshoe, a dog's or horse's head, the Masonic emblem, a clover leaf, his monogram on a plain gold oval, a single jewel such as a ruby—there were hundreds of designs, taking up several pages in the Sears Roebuck catalogue.

For informal, sporting headgear, the faculty wore caps, with a visor. College boys always wore them, and so did small boys. Men wore panamas in summer and black derbies in winter. They lifted them all the way off when they met a lady—"tipping" them. For church, and for "occasions," a gentleman carried a little gold-headed ebony cane. The president of Emory College never went outside his own yard without his.

Either men's hips were not as trustworthy as they became later, or masculine faith was less, for a belt alone was not considered safe enough for such a risk as holding up trousers; suspenders alone gave peace of mind. "Galluses" was the countrified name for them, and prominent on each pair of trousers were eight suspender buttons waiting for them. ("Why do firemen wear red suspenders?" was a favorite riddle.)

Of necessity Mother had to give thought not only to her own

but to her children's clothes, not with the idea of having us in any sort of fashion, but to cover our nakedness, as the Bible would express it, for we grew out of everything, and wore through everything, so fast that she was often really put to it.

Most of our clothes were hand-me-downs from our cousins. Our aunts were thrifty, and held onto things for their own children as long as there was any chance of making them do, and sometimes by the time they got to our legs they were on shaky last legs of their own. Before we could wear them, a patch had to go on. Nobody set out deliberately to look like a tramp, and patches were as inconspicuous as near-matching material and careful sewing could contrive. Blue jeans were worn only by farm workers and the lowest level of laborers; they were not for sport, and their trouser legs would be neatly hemmed, never left ragged.

But to start at the very beginning, with a new baby's clothes. The first ones were aptly called "long clothes," because they certainly were. A tiny new baby's head and little curled hands peeped out of one end of a mass of delicate white dress and several petticoats at least a ridiculous thirty inches long! They provided mothers with plenty of handwork in the way of rolling and whipping ruffles, brierstitching, sewing on rows of insertion and lace edging, making tiny tucks and buttonholes.

Diapers were soft cotton bird's-eye squares, folded first into a triangle, then into a second one, and when the baby's bottom was planked down in the middle of this, the three corners were lapped over each other and safety-pinned. The first announcement to the neighbors that "the little stranger" had arrived was a white billowing back-yard clothesline. On rainy days, diapers hung on clothes racks around the kitchen range, an inconvenience to the cook, to say the least.

When the baby began to stand, and trip itself up on those thirty-inch skirts, it was put into more sensible "short clothes"—

but they were still dainty little handmade white dresses coming down to the ankle. It was only when it was able to scramble around on the floor under its own power that a baby went into practical, machine-stitched colored "rompers"—checked gingham being the favorite material for these.

In summer, small children went barefoot, but in winter there must be high shoes, either laced or buttoned up the side. There was consequently a button-hook in place on every bureau right beside the comb and brush—except when it couldn't be found, and a struggle with a stout wire hairpin had to be substituted. The worst thing of all was to get within a couple of buttons of the top, and discover that you weren't coming out even—evidently you had mismated a button and buttonhole at the very bottom!

The rough Oxford dirt streets were hard on shoes, and three active children were, too. Many a time, when "out in company," I carefully tried to remember to keep the soles of my shoes flat on the floor so no one could see a big hole on the bottom. When a gaping hole first appeared that went all the way through the bottom, we would draw around the shoe on a cardboard, and cut out a sole to fit inside. It didn't last long, unfortunately. A hole would wear in *it*, and then the cardboard would break in two pieces that would stick out of the hole and do its best to trip you. The greatest humiliation was to have one of the worn pieces come all the way out, and people see it.

Women wore lisle stockings, which were all cotton, with a smooth silky finish. Socks were for men and big boys in long pants, not for children. Both boys and girls wore heavy black ribbed long cotton stockings.

We held these heavy stockings up by elastic fasteners pinned to "bodies." Drawers and underskirts buttoned on to these bodies too, and occasionally if buttons came off, or buttonholes were too large, a little girl had the disgrace of an underskirt hanging down and showing. Once at Palmer a third-grade girl stood up to recite and her underskirt fell all the way off. In the course of a long life, she never again distinguished herself in any way, but that was sufficient. She was always remembered as "the girl whose underskirt came off in school." And other members of the family shared the opprobrium: innocent little Henry, two years younger, was known as "the brother of the girl whose underskirt came off in school."

Little girls did not go around in public with neck bones and forearms bare any more than ladies did. If a dress had a low neck and short sleeves, we wore underneath it a white bob-tailed blouse called a guimpe.

We wore our hair in a bob, plaits, or hanging curls—either natural, or else painfully acquired by sleeping on knobs of rags—but always a tremendous wide ribbon bow on top. For dress-up, there was always a white cotton dress, often dotted swiss, which would be set off by a pale blue or pink hair ribbon and a sash to match the hair ribbon tied in a bow in the back. On summer afternoons, when the college president's four young daughters drove past our house, their whole pony-cart seemed to be billowing with white dotted swiss and pastel ribbons.

For everyday use in summer, girls wore common straw hats, with brims to protect their faces from the sun, since "being brown as a berry" was not considered desirable. Sunday hats were sailors, with a ribbon around the crown and streamers hanging down the back. There was one Easter, however, when the two Henderson girls appeared in lace straw hats, one trimmed with pink forget-me-nots and one with blue, and no little girl under twelve gave a thought to the Resurrection.

The days of curls for small boys and Little Lord Fauntleroy suits were fortunately past. The sissiest thing an unfeeling mother could make her little son wear now was a blue or white sailor suit, short tight pants, of course, and a bloused top with a square collar and a triangular dickey buttoned into the neck. For those a little older, for dress-up (which always meant for Sunday school) there was the Norfolk jacket and a Buster Brown collar with its loose, wide bow tie. Ordinarily boys wore percale homemade blouses, and rather tight knee-length pants that had been fashioned from a pair discarded by the head of the house. Boys' hair was cut by the shears in the mothers' sewing baskets. In summer they wore wide-brimmed straw hats, the cheap common variety for field hands, with a shoestring run in and out around the crown. If no hat was available, a boy could tie knots in four corners of a handkerchief and make himself a jaunty, informal sort of head-covering to wear for a job in the sunny yard, or for a sortie with a gang of boys somewhere. In winter, there were skimpy gored cloth caps with small visors, which had the virtue of being so little and so limp that they could be easily crammed into a pocket.

There was no pool or lake anywhere near Oxford, and nobody knew how to swim anyway, so there was no need for the Women's Missionary Society to get themselves into a swivet over the immodesty of bathing suits; there was not a one in town. The little boys who slipped off and dog-paddled in a deep place in Dried Indian Creek did it in a condition known as "nekkid," and on the rare occasions when little girls (without permission, of course) floundered around in knee-deep places somewhere else in the creek, they wore raggedy old dresses or nightgowns, and always kept on some underclothes underneath.

"Doing up" her hair for a girl and "going into long pants" for a boy marked the dividing line between children and "young people." Before that momentous event took place in a girl's life, she had already been inching her way along into young ladyhood by a gradual lowering of the hemline of her dresses. Bobbed hair had been let grow, and by ninth grade, she was confining her hair at the nape of her neck with a barrette. She was still beribboned, but not on top anymore, for the wide bow that had flared up there all these years was now flattened out and pinned straight across the barrette with a hatpin.

Then came the great day on which a girl was adjudged by her parents mature enough—as *she* had thought of herself for some time—to discard ribbon bows altogether and "do up" her hair. In one magnificent sweeping gesture, up it went, and instantly she became a young lady. From then on there was never again a hair bow, but the glory of hairpins, side combs, and back hair.

For a boy, crossing the growing-up line was even more spectacular, for it was done with no premonitory edging along, but in one sensational overnight leap. One day, the trousers were knee-length, and below them, those long black ribbed stockings; the next, he had "gone into long pants" and men's socks. The other boys always pulled up his pantlegs to be sure there weren't the old stockings concealed underneath. Oh yes, there were socks there! There had to be—a pair borrowed from his father's dresser drawer, if he didn't have any of his own yet.

This blissful state was reached when a boy was about fourteen or fifteen, and usually a year after he had been making his parents' lives miserable on the subject. Although for some time already he had appeared to any observer like a great hulk of an overgrown boy, quite prepared for the metamorphosis, when he finally did come forth in the glory of his first pair of long trousers, he suddenly looked like a very small boy in men's clothing.

This was the day for father to take up a position on the hearth rug and remind his son that he was not to smoke before his twenty-first birthday if he wanted to receive the promised watch then, and for mother to go into floods of tears, wailing that they had lost their little boy.

And indeed they had, for once in long pants he was there forever; the Rubicon had been crossed, and there was no going back. The last pair of short trousers started on their trip to Greenland's icy mountains, for the missionary barrel was always gaping, and was the final home for the town's hand-me-downs.

15

Typhoid Fever

The summer I was nine, there was a typhoid fever epidemic. Three children came down with it. The town was scared out of its wits, expecting more cases any day. I was one of the stricken ones, and no one expected me to live. The other two were the Lambert children, at whose house I frequently played, so the water from their well was believed to have been the villain that caused it.

Our vaunted "pure water," about which we constantly bragged, suddenly became suspect: was it possible that it *wasn't* pure? Ladders were immediately lowered into all the town's wells, and men in hip boots went down and sent back up buckets of mud and trash and whatnot. Not only was every well in town scraped clean, but for months all drinking water was boiled, for typhoid was a deadly thing.

I was a very sick child. Two men carried me on a cot up to my grandmother Stone's house, because it was cooler than ours, with an upstairs bedroom with windows on three sides and shaded by a great oak tree. On the way over, having no idea I was considered as good as dead, I was embarrassed to be seen in a nightgown in bed right out in the street, and whenever we passed anyone I drew the sheet over my face, which made for an even more corpse-like appearance.

In due time, the Lambert children pulled through all right, but I almost didn't make it, and wouldn't have if a trained nurse had not been brought down from an Atlanta hospital to take care of me. When fall came, since I was still quite frail, on the doctor's orders I became a school drop-out. At first, wrapped in a quilt in a big chair on the porch, I had long, wonderful days of sitting in the sun and dreaming. My fairy books were a great consolation during those months when all the other children were in school and there was no one to play with and no energy to want to play. On rainy days, I would settle myself comfortably in the old baby cradle by the window in the storeroom, sometimes reading, sometimes just dozing, or watching the rain splash on the panes. I have often wondered if the rest of my life would have been different had it not been for this quiet year of being so much alone to think "the long, long thoughts of youth."

World events as a rule made little impact on Oxford, but during this year there was one great happening that reached even to us— the arrival of Halley's comet. In May 1910, we streamed from our houses to gaze with awe at the comet in the night sky, with its fifty-million-mile-long tail, to marvel at the scientific accuracy that had predicted the exact time that it would appear, and to think of other people in history who had watched it in former centuries— Duke William of Normandy, for one, who had recently stepped ashore on his newly acquired English island. And now *we* were! Someone voiced the sobering thought that only the very young among us standing there had a chance of seeing it when it would come the next time, in 1986. I wondered if I should. It was magnificent enough to be worth staying around for, and I made an inward vow to try to be there.

Eventually, the year passed—the year taken out of my life, when I lost a grade in school. It was a long time before I ceased to resent this, to hold it bitterly against God, instead of being grateful to Him for giving me back my life at all when it so nearly ended.

16

Tales of When the Yankees Came

In the first years of this century, "our little village in the grove" was probably as peaceful a place as existed anywhere on earth. Except for the hourly striking of the big clock on Emory's Seney Hall Tower, and the tinkling of the bells on the collars of the animals that pulled the mulecar, the air was quiet. Professors were undisturbed in their after-dinner hammock naps, hens cackled meditatively to themselves as they crossed the road to see what was on the other side. Slowly moving clouds drifted across the blue overhead, and nothing flew around up there but birds—except perhaps angels, for heaven was straight up.

The thing that made it such a wonderful time in which to be alive was that there was *no fear*. People in town did not go around doing harm to each other. Householders felt no need to lock the door after putting the cat out at night, and if any of them looked under the bed before getting into it, it was pure routine, and not from any expectation of finding anybody there. The newspapers were not a daily catalogue of horrors. Any terrible happenings were accidents, not planned deliberately by wicked men who came eagerly forward to "take the credit" for having caused them. It was unimaginable that another nation might without warning not only wipe us off the face of the earth, but destroy the whole world as well.

Of course there was always Judgment Day in the offing, but the warning about that had been sounded for so many hundreds of years with nothing happening that it no longer alarmed. And besides, weren't we the "good guys," the sheep, who were going to be saved? As long as we behaved ourselves as good church members, we would have nothing to worry about when this touted biblical cataclysm did come. A little local war around the corner was much more to be feared.

But wars were over; there weren't going to be any more. There *had* been one, and of such importance and of such consequences to our section of the country that ever after we dated events "before the war" almost as we did B.C. But everyone was positive that no one now living would ever see war again.

Covington had been right in the path of Sherman's march to Savannah from Atlanta, but because it was the hometown of one of his West Point friends, he had given orders that it was not to be touched. Oxford was not so fortunate. One might think that so unpretentious a little village of Methodist preachers and teachers would hardly attract the attention of an invading army, but nothing was safe from the Yankee invaders. It was a few miles out of the direct line of Sherman's path, but in 1864 it was the target of an afternoon's raid. Almost every house in Oxford was pillaged.

At the Branhams', one of the invaders rode his horse through the open front door and into the hall where Mrs. Branham was standing. She informed him curtly that the stables were in the rear, and added her opinion of Yankees in general. Furious, he threatened to burn the house down "to teach her a lesson," but a northern woman, a teacher at Palmer who was boarding there, persuaded him to spare it. When he ordered "Aunt" Aggie, the cook, to prepare a meal immediately for him and ten of his men, the unruffled old woman put her hands on her hips and told him, "Yawl'll jes' have to wait. The white folks ain't et yet."

Mrs. Williams's home was one of the few that escaped the Yankees' thieving fingers. When she heard that enemy soldiers were in Covington, and were headed for Oxford, she tacked a large piece of red cloth on a porch pillar and sat down in a rocker near it to await them. They dashed into the yard, and asked the meaning of the red cloth. "Smallpox," she said, and they galloped on.

Two places in the town remain to be pointed out to visitors as mementos of that terrible time.

One was the Griffin house—our house now—where the Confederate girl spy had safely hidden from the Yankee patrol that came "to hang her if they found her, and to burn the house that sheltered her." While Sherman was burning Atlanta, Izora Fair was living in Oxford, a refugee from Charleston. The Confederates were anxious to know what his next move would be, and Izora volunteered to try to find out. Staining her face with walnut juice, cutting off her hair and kinking up the rest with tongs, she disguised herself as a black woman and made her way on foot forty miles to the Yankee camp. There for a few days she represented herself as looking for a worthless husband who had run away to join the blue-clad army, meandering good-naturedly around the camp, joking with the men, telling fortunes, helping out with the cooking and washing, and keeping her ears open. When she learned what she needed to know, she returned to Oxford and described her adventure and its resulting information in a letter to the governor of Georgia. The letter was in the Oxford post office, waiting to go, when a band of skirmishers looted the post office and took the mail sacks to their camp. Sherman immediately sent a party of soldiers back to find the girl.

She was boarding at the Griffin house, and hid under the rafters in a dark crawl-space whose opening was hidden when the door

Confederate Cemetery

to one of the little second-floor bedrooms was opened out into the hall. The person who conducted the searching party through the entire house threw open all the doors freely to show them that nothing was being hidden, and stood with her back against this little door. The crawl-space was never discovered. A historical marker in front of the house now tells the whole story.

The other surviving memento of "the late unpleasantness" is the little war cemetery. There were no classes at the college during most of the years of the fighting. Students—the senior class to a man—were in the army, and the deserted buildings were used as a hospital for some of the wounded in the battle of Atlanta. When Sherman's men came through Georgia, they tore up the railroad tracks as they passed, so hospital supplies sorely needed at both Covington and Oxford hospitals could no longer come in, and the wounded often became the dead. There was no transportation to take their bodies home, so those who died in the college buildings had to be buried in town. Their graves were dug in the pine woods behind the college chapel, and the little cemetery remains as a permanent reminder of Oxford's part in those heartbreaking years. Regulation military headstones were later erected over the graves—twenty-five bearing the names of the men buried beneath them, seven marked "unknown." They are for both Confederate and Union men.

The people of Oxford did not forget them. On every Memorial Day there were exercises at the church, and the best orator among the schoolboys recited "The Blue and the Gray," "The Sword of Robert E. Lee," or that heartbreaker, "Little Giffen of Tennessee." Then came a solemn procession to the little cemetery in the woods, the white-clad schoolgirls carrying wreaths of cedar and roses they had made for the graves of the long-ago young soldiers who were brought here to die.

> Under the sod and the dew,
> Waiting the Judgment Day,
> Tears and love for the Blue,
> Love and tears for the Gray.

17

It Was the Best of Times . . .

If everybody stayed well, our simple life was idyllic, but when illness came, it was another story. We had one great advantage; doctors, bless their hearts, like grocery clerks, made house calls. But to get hold of one in the first place was the problem. Someone had to run, bicycle, saddle a horse, or hitch up a buggy to summon him. In the meantime, in an emergency the patient might and sometimes did die.

Our nearest physician was in Covington. To be sure, that was not strictly true; there was another one in Oxford, an elderly man, who had few patients. Perhaps because of unhappiness over his small practice, he had taken refuge in his drug cabinet and become that fearful thing then called "a dope fiend." Most Oxford people did not dare trust themselves to his diagnosis or prescriptions, which they said might only be colored water. He could not afford to keep a horse, and unless his black and rural patients came for him in a wagon, he would go to them on foot, even several miles in the country, proving himself, if not too skillful as a physician, at least a saint in kindness.

But what was the first thing that even our trusted Covington doctor was almost sure to prescribe for every ailment? Calomel, than which there was nothing more horrible. If you weren't already sick, you certainly were after you had taken a dose of it.

We relied on our good air, pure water, and alcohol-free town for continued health, never bothering with physical check-ups. What would be the point of going to a doctor when there was nothing the matter with you?

Even if one were suspected of not being perfectly well, the doctor wasn't always called. There were a few standard remedies that mothers administered, after a hand laid on your forehead decided whether or not you were feverish. Castoria was not bad, although we certainly never lived up to the manufacturer's claim that "children cry for it." There was a druggist's saturnine mixture of iron, quinine, and strychnine, which between them surely had the strength to vanquish every possible ill. There was a heavy white oily syrup like wallpaper paste (only tasting much worse) called Somebody-or-Other's Emulsion, supposed to be for "wasting diseases." If my mother got the idea into her head that we weren't bouncing around quite as actively as usual, she ladled out a spoonful of that loathsome stuff. It always worked: we bounced immediately in order to make sure we got no more. If your tongue was white ("coated"), it meant that you were bilious, and calomel was on the way.

There was no drugstore closer than Covington (called familiarly "Cuv" by Emory students and most Oxonians), and its shelves told plainly what its relatively few medications were for: corn plasters, wart removers, Arnica salve for cuts and bruises, Cascarets—gentle, safe, and certain bowel cleansers—Lydia Pinkham's Vegetable Compound and Cardui for women's complaints.

We never had dental check-ups. A few drops of oil of cloves or the application of a warm pillow would temporarily soothe a toothache. If it continued and became unbearable, people went to an Atlanta dentist. From pure neglect many people had false teeth.

Few grown-ups and no children wore eyeglasses. There was not a single pair, belonging either to teachers or to students, at Palmer

Institute. Glasses were really glass, and if dropped, even on a rug, would usually shatter. Regular spectacles had gun-metal or gold wire rims. A few people who needed glasses only for close work wore the more dandified pince-nez.

Children went barefooted in the summer, and mosquitoes and flies bit their bare legs. When we scratched the bites with our dirty little hands, sores resulted. Then we wet a piece of paper and stuck it on the sore, and left it there until the sore healed, and the paper peeled off of itself. When the famous Jack fell down and broke his crown, he had vinegar and brown paper, but we used water and any sort of paper that was handy—strips of it torn out of a tablet if we were at school, wet with that useful, ever-present product, spit.

As a result of going barefooted, boys almost always had badly stubbed toes. A sore, bloody toe had a narrow strip torn from an old sheet wound around it, and then the two ends were crossed and carried around the ankle to be tied, in the hope that it would stay on. Dusty sidewalks and streets soon made it filthy dirty, bedraggled, and utterly revolting. Why boys didn't all have gangrene and their feet cut off is a mystery.

There were no screens on houses. On summer nights, if the season had been rainy and mosquitoes were active, there were canopy nets hung over the beds, and people slept inside their protection. Sometimes a mosquito sneaked under first. Mosquito netting was often tacked over a kitchen window, for it was there that flies congregated.

Except around food, flies were not very bothersome, but in dining rooms and kitchens they occasioned a constant battle. Sheets of flypaper were spread about with sticky yellow glue that was irresistible to flies. Down they zoomed to the delectable feast, and their legs and wings stuck fast. A piece of flypaper that had been on duty for some time was not an appetizing sight. This deadly paper was also made in long thin strips that could dangle from a doorway—perfect to run into in the dark.

To keep off the flies while a meal was in progress, quite often there waved over the dining room table either a little branch with fluttering leaves from a peach tree or a bamboo wand with strips of paper attached. In boardinghouses and country hotels, if a small boy from the kitchen department were available, he would stand at one end of the table and work at gently pulling on a long string attached to this sort of "shoo-fly" fan, which was hung over the table like a chandelier.

House flies were small black things, annoying but not too detestable. The flies that hung around the privies were something else. They were larger, like horseflies, iridescent, and looked poisonous, as indeed they were.

It was the era of fans, and with them we confronted whatever summer weather the good Lord sent us. Porch sitters and church congregations solemnly flapped fans to keep off the flies and to cool themselves. For sedate people there were large straw-colored palmetto fans made out of a single leaf, dried and bound around the edge to keep it from splitting, or silk stretched on an ebony frame with a Japanese scene painted on the silk. Pasteboard fans were left in church seats, with advertising pictures of young ladies taking snuff, drinking Coca-Cola, or holding an armful of cornstalks that were going to be made into Kellogg's Corn Flakes. Belles used decorated folding paper or silk fans for flirting.

Between children and grown-ups there was a distinct line of separation, and to all on the older side of that line respect was due and was paid. Anyone who was our elder was automatically considered our better. Never was so heinous a thing done as to call grown people, especially one's parents, by their given names. My cousin Sara, whom adults dubbed "a saucy little minx," audaciously called her father "Dad," and right to his face, too, but not another child in town presumed to be that flip. It was Father and Mother, Papa and Mama. The Victorian pronunciation of Pa-*pa* and Ma-*ma* had been abandoned, however; it was as if they had been spelled *Popper* and *Mommer*. Grown-up cousins were always given a respectful prefix, such as Cousin Ruth, Cousin Johnnie.

There was no open, blatant vulgarity. We were reticent about intimate physical affairs. Parts of our bodies were spoken of—or rather, *not* spoken of—as "privates," and they were considered as such and did not figure in conversation. If a young lady had to retire for any reason, she said she had "to powder her nose." Four-letter words were words with four letters—lamb, dish, plan, rose. The word s-e-x existed neither in conversation nor in print. We were not unrealistic enough to believe that there was no vulgarity or sin around us; we only hoped that they would be recognized for the shameful things they were, and not vaunted or made familiar by being brought openly into conversation.

When we went over to the county seat, we sometimes saw such words written on the sides of freight cars standing on the switch-tracks, probably done by a tramp. For there were tramps—dirty, ragged, homeless men, often made that way by alcohol, who crawled into empty boxcars, and sometimes came into the towns along the railroad to knock at doors and ask for handouts, or remove pies left cooling in the kitchen windows or clothes sunning and airing on a line in the back yard. Oxford's distance from a railroad made us safe from these loose-livers and their panhandling.

Middle-class people did not travel much; a trip on the train was the height of adventure. Train seats were liberally sprinkled with cinders, lying large and black and rough and cruel on the red plush seats, for the locomotives burned coal, and anybody who felt he was suffocating could open the window and let in, besides fresh air, a wave of black smoke and a whole bombardment of cinders. They grated as you sat on them, but it was your eyes that they made for unerringly. Never did a person take even a short train trip without being assaulted by at least one. Mother always took along in her reticule a little packet of flax seed from the drugstore to get them out. The idea was to put in your eye a whopping big flax seed, which attached itself to the cinder. Tears pushed it to the edge, and then they would be wiped out together. It was easier to remove a beam than a mote.

At the front of the train coach was a painted tin watercooler, with a "common cup" chained to it. Mother was ahead of her time in not allowing us to drink from this. Whenever we went anywhere on the train, she always took along my oldest brother's silver baby cup. (As the first baby, he had received many such presents; friends' enthusiasm waned as the rest of us kept coming, and there were no more silver cups.) After the family had been refreshed, Mother would be pretty sure to feel that the cuttings that she was taking to Aunt Emma or her grandmother on such a long trip (forty miles!) needed a little sprinkling to keep them fresh, so again the cup made a trip to the watercooler. No one from Oxford ever went "abroad" without a little damp box of cuttings on her knees as an offering to her hostess.

It was a rare person who took a real trip abroad—meaning out of the United States, and if so, it was pretty sure to be his only one. Rich New York people whom we read about, but did not know, went to Europe on "the grand tour," and musicians and medical students studied in Germany, but most of us traveled only in armchairs with *Stoddard's Lectures*. The trips we did take were always to visit nearby relatives. We never stayed in a hotel.

The people who traveled to the Orient were missionaries, and when they went, it was usually for good. There would be a farewell service at the church that resembled a funeral more than anything else, and we sang dolefully, "Jesus, I my cross have taken, all to leave and follow Thee." Although a few missionaries might come back years later to go around on speaking tours at churches, most spent their entire lives "in the mission field," coming home at last so old, so worn, that they were not recognizable as the eager, dedicated young people, shining with zeal and enthusiasm, who had gone away. They married each other out there, and then had to part with their children as they sent them back to American colleges, where they always took all the honors, having had an excellent early foundation training in the mission schools with no frills and worldly distractions.

There were no billboards defacing the scenery, and to take a country buggy ride was a real refreshment for the spirit. Of course there were occasional accidents due to runaway horses, but at least thousands of people were not killed or mangled each year by collisions between buggies or farm wagons. There were no newspaper headlines that 785 persons had been killed on the roads over a holiday weekend.

No one would willingly go back to the bother and danger of kerosene lamps, to the labor and tedium of drawing up water bucket by bucket from a well, to bowl and pitcher baths, and to traipsing the length of the back yard to get to the toilet on a rainy winter night. These inconveniences certainly made it the worst of times. But didn't the gentle peace of those slow-moving days in that slow-moving town also make it the best of times?

18

Vale!

Atlanta was our nearest city, and our lodestar. When Oxford boys and girls finished their education and wanted a broader field in which to maneuver, it was to Atlanta they looked. So when the time came that Mother had to admit that a few boarding students and occasional dress-making were not meeting the bills for a family of four, and that some other way must be found, it was to Atlanta that she took us.

Before her marriage she had been a stenographer in Macon, and now she fell back upon those skills mastered almost twenty years before. She went again through the Pittman shorthand books she had studied in the Kentucky business school; she rented a typewriter, and soon her fingers, stiffened by housework, picked up their old nimbleness and were flying over the keys.

Leaving Oxford would mean taking both boys out of college, and although this almost broke my mother's heart, she told herself that it would only be for a year or two. With the three of them working, surely the debts she had had to make, which seemed a great load to her but were actually not tremendous, could be paid off within a few years, and then the boys' education would be taken up again. The older one needed only one more year to be graduated; the younger one had just matriculated as a sub-freshman. Not to be both an Emory graduate and a Kappa Alpha was an unthinkable thing in our family.

My older brother already knew about the proposed move, for he and Mother always talked things over and made plans together, and he had helped her review her shorthand by dictating in the evenings after we younger ones were in bed. One night after supper, Mother broke the news to Harry and me. It came as a terrific surprise and shock. At first, the idea of *leaving Oxford, our home*, the *center of the universe*, was devastating, but soon, callous little brat that I was, I began to see it as a great adventure, and Harry, ever the money-getter, really looked forward to having a full-time job and a weekly salary instead of studying physics and Latin.

Mother had had a few necessary pieces of furniture crated to follow us by freight car, and at the end of the college year, for the last time (and the first, too), she locked the door of the house that had been our home for eight years. Carrying our valises and grips, we boarded the mulecar for the railway at Covington. Just after the "up train" crossed the Yellow River bridge, we had from its windows a last glimpse of the Emory clock tower, showing above the campus oaks.

Everybody in Oxford had relatives in Atlanta with whom they stayed as a matter of course whenever they were there overnight, or, if they were thinking of moving there, while they were looking around. My family's base was the home of one of my father's sisters, who was childless, had a big house, and was comfortably enough off to be able to show hospitality to any relatives or out-of-town friends. Three young Oxford nephews, working in Atlanta, were a permanent part of the household, and even the cook, who had been brought to Atlanta by my aunt years before, had a roomy apartment in the basement where her Shakerag friends visiting the city were made welcome.

So we went first to Aunt Emma's for a few days, and she and her husband kindly bestirred themselves in getting us settled— Uncle Howard to help find jobs for Mother and Harry, and Aunt

Seney Hall Tower

Emma to locate a little house for us to rent, near enough for their home to be something of a second home for me between the time when my school was out at 2:00 and when Mother got home from her office at 5:30. Although my aunt herself was often not there, as she was involved in many church and social engagements, there were three servants, so the house was always open. But as it worked out, I was a little drunk with my new independence, and often, rather than going to her house, I went instead to the home of a schoolmate for the afternoon or to our own empty house. At the age of eleven, a sixth-grader, I became a "latchkey kid."

We were living out on the edge of Atlanta, but again, as in Oxford, the streetcar went almost by our door. This time it was not a little yellow vehicle passing four times a day, and drawn by mules with jingling bells, but long, sophisticated cars connected by a trolley to an electric cable overhead, and after dark, blazing with electric lights. The streetcar came every ten minutes, and Mother and Harry rode it to work every day.

The modest little house that Aunt Emma had found for us seemed to me to be a wonderful place, for it was lighted by gas (new to me) and had city waterworks, which meant no more trips outdoors, and the splendor of a big white bathtub. Another thing that made a great impression upon me were the paved sidewalks, where children sped along on a marvelous mode of travel of which I had never heard, roller skates. A public grammar school was only a fifteen-minute walk away, and I joined the neighborhood children who streamed there. Almost at once, I found among them that necessity of a little girl's life, a best friend, and was soon writing bragging letters back to Mary about my new school and the delights of Atlanta.

For Mother, the delights included a Methodist church near us, finding work immediately in the same building with my uncle (this seemed to her "safer"), and a job for fifteen-year-old Harry in the mailing room of the telephone company. (He stayed with the company all his life, working in places as far-flung as New Orleans and New York City, and wound up as a vice-president.)

When Harry took this first job, he was still in short pants. After their third payday, he and Mother clubbed together and bought him a long-pants suit. He wore it out of the store, and did not come home for several hours, strolling up and down Whitehall and Peachtree streets, admiring himself in the store windows and giving Atlanta citizens the same opportunity. An elderly man put his hand on the shoulder of the new suit.

"Your first long pants, son?"

Harry admitted that that was the case.

"Let me give you a tip; take the price tag off the right pants leg."

For the three of us in Atlanta, together every evening around the familiar dining room table, talking of dear old Oxford, and having interesting new experiences to tell each other, life was happy enough, but my older brother's situation was a lonely and sad one. Not only was he missing his senior year and his degree, but months of searching in Atlanta had turned up no work that promised anything, and the best he could finally find was the position of principal in a little country school. It was many miles away in South Georgia, and to a serious, sensitive seventeen-year-old boy, it seemed a long way from everything he had known and loved.

And back in Oxford, what was happening? We were homesick for our old home, but did it even miss us? There was certainly no great cataclysm because of our going, and the small gaps we left in its life were soon filled. Another boy was easily found to deliver the Atlanta evening newspapers, and some other woman (not quite so easily, perhaps) was persuaded to take over the children's missionary society. Certainly the village life moved quietly on as usual for a while.

But only for a while; a great change was coming to the college, and so to the whole town that revolved around it.

Mr. Asa Candler, the Coca-Cola tycoon, who had sent all his

sons to Emory, had for some time had his eye on the college, and envisioned a glorious future for it. He now offered a breathtaking million dollars if it would move to Atlanta. This magnificent offer certainly put the cat among the pigeons!

There was heated controversy over whether to accept its conditions or not. Not everybody among those who had anything to do with the management of the college believed that bigger was necessarily better; it might be decidedly worse. Many held out stoutly against such a drastic thing as moving away from Oxford. Was a city environment preferable to a rural one for young men during this critical stage of their development?

But a *million dollars*, in one lump sum!

To be the recipient of this magnificent gift, or not to be, that was the question that was wrenching the college apart, and setting old friends and colleagues in opposite camps. Should the college continue in the pleasant path that for almost a hundred years had proved eminently satisfactory, or tear itself violently up by the roots? Was it true that Emory was being held captive by the past, when a dazzling future might be possible? All those dollars were so tempting; what could not be done with them?

After long months of soul-searching and often bitter debate, it was decided to accept the gift, and make the move. For the second time in its history, Emory bravely started from scratch. Impressive new college buildings rose in a sea of red mud among the pines on the outskirts of Atlanta, as Emory was born again, and the little liberal arts country college of several hundred boys began its spectacular bean-stalk growth to become a great university, with thousands of students pursuing many disciplines.

In this case, bigger *has* proved to be better. The right decision was rewarded when in 1979 the Coca-Cola Company topped Mr. Candler's first million with another gift of a hundred and five million dollars, the largest gift ever made to any college, anywhere, in the history of the world. And what *couldn't* be done with that amount?

The beloved little campus of the early years was not forgotten, however, but given a bite of the Coca-Cola pie. Renovated and enlarged, it became Oxford College, one of the many schools of the new university, where approximately five hundred coeds study for the first two years of their Emory bachelor's degree. Among its new buildings are dormitories sufficient to house them all, so no longer is it the custom of Oxford families "to have a few boys."

Goodrich White, president of the new university, and an alumnus of the old Emory, said in an address at Oxford, "No one who has ever lived in this blessed town can speak of it without emotion."

The last word: Oxford, blessed town!